THE CRITICAL ATTITUDE

THE
CRITICAL ATTITUDE

BY

FORD MADOX FORD

Essay Index Reprint Series

Originally published by:

DUCKWORTH & CO.

BOOKS FOR LIBRARIES PRESS, INC.
FREEPORT, NEW YORK

First published 1911
Reprinted 1967

LIBRARY OF CONGRESS CATALOG CARD NUMBER:
67-30187

PRINTED IN THE UNITED STATES OF AMERICA

TO

W. P. KER

THE momentarily paralysing thought occurs to me that this page must appear flat hypocrisy—for is not hypocrisy the homage paid to virtue by vice? And, when I consider the sheer levity, the unbridled licence of appraisement of the Great and the Serious that is contained in some of the pages that follow, truly I sit appalled at the consideration : for how shameless must such pages appear, thus brought into immediate contact with a name standing in all places for the serious and high purpose of thought more orthodox and more controlled. Nevertheless, it is with all sincerity that I inscribe myself Professor Ker's very humble, obliged servant,

THE AUTHOR.

v

CONTENTS

ON THE OBJECTION TO
THE CRITICAL ATTITUDE

THE
CRITICAL ATTITUDE

CHAPTER I

INTRODUCTORY

ON THE OBJECTION TO THE CRITICAL ATTITUDE

I

THE essays of which the following book is made up were contributed originally to the *English Review*. It has been objected in several respectable quarters that these pages rang the changes too continuously upon a certain set of names, and the objection for what it is worth is a very respectable one. But the end of the ass is to draw carts, the end of the respectable journal is to limit thought within the bounds of respectability; the end of the hyena is to disinter from graveyards the great bones which with its powerful jaws it crushes, extracting no doubt succulent marrow. So the *English Review* had its purposes and its ends. Its end— as far as its original purpose was concerned—was peace, though in its old shape and with a spirit much more beloved it flourishes like a blue bay tree. Its purposes were several, chief amongst these being the furthering of a certain school of literature and of a certain tone of thought. There is a considerable writer—once he wrote the best short stories that are to be found in English literature, now, alas! *il pontifie*—there is a certain writer who once said that he welcomed the coming of the motor car because it would make the Englishman think. We confess to having always been unable to get at the inner significance of this phrase. One motor car might take an Englishman to Brighton, but could ten thousand make him think? Assuredly not, for nothing could make him think; nothing could make him review his thoughts. The ass draws his cart; the respectable journal preaches respectability; the hyena disinters and crunches his bones; but the Englishman—he is just God's Englishman.

So that an *English Review* is a contradiction in terms: it was—as far as the original purpose of its two founders was concerned—also a splendid, forlorn hope. It set out to do what that eminent writer said would be the function of the motor car. But no sane man would set out to make the ass play upon a musical instrument, the respectable journal to take broad views, or the hyena to distil eau-de-cologne. For these things upon the face of them would be insane enterprises. So with the *English Review*, which set out to enjoin upon the Englishman a critical attitude.

4

OBJECTION TO THE CRITICAL ATTITUDE

But nothing will make the Englishman adopt a critical attitude. He is a sentient being, he can feel ; he is a poietic being, he can act ; he is a poetic one, has he not given us the finest verse of the modern world ? Sartorially he is without an equal on earth. He is, in fact, constructive. Luther and Darwin between them have destroyed revealed religion except for the few belated souls who linger in the folds of the Churches of Rome, of Greece, of Mohammed, of Buddha and the rest. But for his own particular islands, where Luther and Darwin like consecutive steam-rollers extinguished by force of criticism all possibility of simple faith, the Englishman has founded three hundred and forty-seven religions. And each of these religions is founded upon a compromise. That is what the Englishman does to, that is how he floors—the critical attitude.

In these islands critics have been extraordinarily rare. When they have arisen they have been listened to with dislike and dread, with a show of respect. Then they have been petted out of the way. If a slug should enter a bee-hive, these industrious insects will, if they can accomplish it, slay him with their stings, but failing this and in any case they set to work and cover him with wax. They pack the wax down, they smooh it over ; they extinguish, in fact, that poor slug until he reposes beneath a fair monument, a respectable protuberance from which escape neither groans nor foul odours. Now our islands are the bee-hives, and what is the critic in England

5

when, direfully, he appears but just a slug ? He lives
if he has a chance, suspected, dreaded, applauded
Then he disappears. He is covered with the wax of
oblivion. So it has been with, let us say, Hobbes,
Matthew Arnold, and Mr Ruskin, who being dead are
nearly as much forgotten as the inventor of the
safety bicycle.

II

The English consumer of the arts limits himself in
his criticism to saying that such and such a book is a
good book, such and such a picture is a good picture,
or such and such a piece of music is a good piece of
music. This means to say either that he likes the
book, or that he thinks that he ought to say that he
likes the book, the picture, or the piece of music. Or,
on the other hand, he will substitute for the epithet
" good " that of " bad." This means that he dislikes the
work in question, or considers that he ought to ` say
that he dislikes it. And this is not the critical attitude.

On the other hand it is not a criminal attitude.
Theoretically considered a good work of art would
be one that every proper man would like. Thus
" The Victory of Samothrace " will by some be considered the supreme work of art. By others it will
be loved in a lesser degree. But it is inconceivable
to imagine any human being—or at any rate any
occidental—who would dislike it. But if, on the other
hand, we take the Holy Scriptures, we find a work

that, by a considerable portion of Christendom, is considered the book of books. It is beloved, it is pored over, it is learned by heart, it inspires heroisms, devotions, or cruelties. This is the case with Protestants and the children of Protestants, who take in its teachings from their births, and by its standards measure good and evil. But Roman Catholics and free-thinkers approach the Bible with an attitude much more critical, and find in it barbarisms, crudenesses, disproportions, and revelations of sickening cruelties. We ourselves, going by accident—and in consequence with livelier perceptions—into an Anglican place of worship, have been horrified and revolted by the extracts from the Bible which were read to a congregation of apparently amiable and humane persons. The extract from the New Testament dealt with eternal fire, that from the Old recounted how a Jewish king had a place of worship surrounded by his soldiers and all the worshippers butchered. Afterwards he sat in a gateway and had the heads of the worshippers cast down before him, each head wrapped up in a palm leaf for convenience of carriage. And this history was so exceedingly well done in a literary sense that, although we are personally too little acquainted with the Scriptures to re-discover this passage, and although the occasion was many years ago, it remains vividly fixed in our memory.

Here at once the question of criticism steps in. That the Bible renders its scenes with extraordinary literary skill practically no one would care to deny. But whereas on the one hand the good Protestant will call it the book of books, and will for the matter of that say that all good English finds its inspiration from the English translation of the Scriptures, it is perfectly open to the good Catholic to consider that the Bible is a disagreeably realistic book. The militant atheist—if any militant atheists still remain —will consider it a horrible work enshrining the most deleterious, the most immoral doctrines. The purely indifferent man alone could consider the Bible with a perfectly open mind, and with a perfectly open mind criticise alike its subject-matter and its literary value.

No one, on the other hand, could criticise the moral subject of " The Winged Victory." It has receded ; we have advanced into regions of an entire aloofness, so that all we have to consider and all it offers us to consider are the sweep of the great wings, the wind in the folds of the dress, the forward poise of the incomparable body. It is to a position of some such aloofness that, in writing " The Critical Attitude," we have attempted to attain. So to achieve, from such a distance to view the things that are around us, is perhaps the most difficult task in life. On the one hand we have our friendships, on the other our quarrels ; on the one side are our preferences and hopes, on the other our vision of things as they are. For nothing is more difficult, nothing is more terrible than to look things in the face. We have to be ready to recognise, and if we are strong enough to acclaim, that things seeming to us hideous may embody a New Beauty. We have to watch modern life sweeping away the traditions that we love, the places that we considered hallowed ; we have to consider that it is blowing away us ourselves as if we were no more than a little dust. And yet, if we have consciences, we must seek to perceive order in this disorder, beauty in what shocks us, and premonitions of immortality in that which sweeps us into forgotten graves.

And this is the hardest task of all. For, rightly considered, criticism which has in it the essentials of valid criticism is not only a disintegrator, is not only destructive, does not even only restrain. If it cannot be constructive it should at least exhort : if, on the one hand, it must say, " Examine into the composition and the past history of your pill before you swallow it," on the other hand, once the composition and this history are ascertained to be satisfactory, it must enjoin with no doubting voice the deglutition. Therefore the critical attitude is so much disliked, is so much distrusted by humanity.

For we have all of us our little panaceas, our little beliefs, our little dogmas ; and for each of these panaceas, beliefs, and dogmas we desire a certain tenderness of handling. They are the integral portion of our being ; they are ourselves more than are the members of our body ; they are the things for which we would go to the death more willingly than for the

9

roof which shelters our heads. Anon comes the critic. He professes to be ready to weigh in the balance not only the panaceas of ourselves and of our friends, but also the pretensions of those who are our opponents. He pretends to do justice between cause and cause as equally as the backbone of the herring lies amid most of the fish. And this appears to us a pestilential proposition—for we desire that those ideas which are a part of ourselves, which are our very selves—that those ideas should be treated with some of the tenderness which is due to divine things. For are we not, being the children of God, divine ? Thus the approach of the critic is chilling. It is not so much that we object to justice being done to our opponent : it is that for our very existence we must in our weak places have the benefit of the doubt. It is not enough that the critic should say that we are nine parts gold to one part dross, for that one part will be to us dearest of all. It is not enough that the critics will say to us as writer that we have not in the world, in all space, or in all time our equal for what is called " getting an atmosphere," since we desire to be praised for our rendering of the emotion of railway travelling or of the passion of love. And indeed it is not only for this that we hate the critic. He may censure our actions and leave us unmoved ; he may condemn what we have produced and only spur us to the effort to produce better. But what we dread is that he may demonstrate to ourselves the hollowness of our beliefs. Our adversary may outvote us ; he may burn us at the stake, but he will not touch the dogmas that give warmth to our heart and directness to our glance. But the critic, praising us upon the one hand, may on the other put into our hearts the doubt not only of ourselves but of our leaders ; he may take all the comfort out of life. The good Christian, that is to say, dislikes comparatively little the pagan who says that he should be burnt for his beliefs. But, if a critical, dispassionate, a cold-blooded student should demonstrate—supposing it to be demonstrable—that the Redeemer was fallible, this critic would be immensely more disliked. He would be shuddered at : his name would be anathema. M. Anatole France, that is to say, who explains away the miracles of Blessed Joan, whilst admiring her heroism, her self-sacrifice, and her military genius—M. Anatole France would have been much more disliked by the supporters of the maid than the persons who burned her. He would have been disliked more deeply and more fundamentally, since he would have caused a greater trouble of the heart. Or again, an ironfounder might, with the vapours from his chimney, shut out the light of the sun for a great number of us, and we should not do much more than grumble. But should the same man attempt to demonstrate that the sun was not the centre of the solar system, we should at once be filled by an enormous and a contagious dread, for he would be attacking one of our settled ideas. The tendency of humanity is to give to all its settled ideas an equal value, and most men upon hearing the theory of the solar system attacked would exclaim : " What next ? " for they would foresee that by encouraging this one iconoclast, they would be opening the door to men who would desire to test and to shake all other accepted ideas. If the sun were dethronable, so also they would feel would be the British Constitution, British family life, the law of marriage, and the very laws of property themselves.

And this is true in every sphere of criticism. It is generally accepted that Milton was a great poet, and that Dr Johnson was no writer but a gross talker, whose remarks were taken down by Mr Boswell. Now, supposing that a critic should arise to say that " Paradise Lost " is a dull and pompous work, and that the figure of Milton, by obscuring the less-known seventeenth-century poets, has shut our eyes to a whole world of lyrical beauty for which all the epics and all the prose writing of Milton can never make amends, all men with their accepted ideas on a literary hierarchy will exclaim against the impertinence or the very atheism of the critic. And this indignation, this moral fervour will be felt by men whose affection for the works of Milton is of the most mediocre. For here again mankind will say, " Where will this end ? "

The fact is that a man of action feels that he cannot with assurance pursue the course marked out for him by his will if his intellect be troubled by doubts.

OBJECTION TO THE CRITICAL ATTITUDE

Upon the face of it one would say that mankind, seeking as it does for novelties, would welcome new ideas, would find in them something fresh, something delightful, something interesting. But this is not the case. The fact is that new ideas almost invariably affect our sense of values—our sense of the whole values of everything. If you tamper with the ideal of the marriage laws you will interfere not only with the sanctity of the home, but also with the sense of property, with values in literature, and with all ideas of human relationship. To interfere with these ideas is very seriously to diminish the motive force that impels men to any protracted and consistent course of action. For most men commit themselves to action, not for the sake of the action itself, but in order to attain to some end altogether extraneous. A man will work honestly, industriously, soberly, in work that has no particular interest for him—and this fortunately or unfortunately is the lot of the great majority of Englishmen; he will undertake painful labours, he will perfect arduous undertakings, not for the love of those pains and labours, but in order to attain to the exclusive society of some woman, to decorate her with stuffs and furs, memorial of his prowess, to establish his children work-free in a working world, to acquire acres upon which he may set his feet, saying, " This from the peak of heaven to the centre of the world is my own."

If, then, the critic shall say that the perfect union between man and woman is a thing so rare that the greatest good of the greatest number demands the abolition of the institution of marriage, this man of action will feel sub-consciously, though he will not put it into words, that he is weakened, that strength has gone out from him. He will not listen to the critic ; if it be practicable he will stone him to death. For, by depriving him of that single-minded necessity for exertion, the critic will have deprived him of so much vital force.

III

Thus in lands whose inhabitants are principally men of action, the critical attitude is almost more disliked and almost more distrusted by the looker-on than by the subject of the criticism, since the desire of men of action is to get something done. This desire accounts for the English doctrine of muddling through in matters of State. It accounts also in matters of art for the fact that very rarely has the English artist in whatever branch he practises any considerable technical excellence. He trusts so much more to temperament ; and just as the British statesman very seldom studies such things as history, or the psychology of crowds, so, practically never— except in very limited circles or during limited periods —does the English artist make any technical studies beyond what are absolutely necessary for the elementary practice of his art.

And, indeed, the English nation demands of its

statesmen, as of its artists, this quality of amateurish-
ness. For its Cabinet ministers it demands qualities,
not of the head, but of the heart ; and it asks the same
of its preachers as of its painters, from its statesmen
as from its authors. For in England, a cool, clear-
headed, and remorseless lawgiver would be regarded
with as much misgiving and dislike as would be a
novelist of the type of Guy de Maupassant. Yet,
essentially the function of a law is to eliminate,
scientifically, certain elements of the body-politic
that other elements may be encouraged, and essentially the function of the novel is to render life, even
though its ultimate aim should be to make life a
better thing.

England, however, has hardly ever produced a
remorseless novelist. Smollett is perhaps the one
example that she can show, and for one lover of
Smollett in the land, Sterne, who wilfully and even
cynically sentimentalised over human vicissitudes,
can show ten thousand. England has practically
never produced a remorseless statesman. Thomas
Cromwell is almost the only example that she can
show. Yet, for one person who does not revile the
name of the Flail of the Monks—and none can be
found to love him !—there are hundreds of thousands
who praise the ghost of Cromwell's kinsman, Oliver.
Yet, the Lord Protector, a mighty military organiser,
was as a statesman a pale and ineffectual employer
of the tremendous force that his great-uncle had put
ready to his hand. For, not only did Thomas Cromwell

15

render a return to Catholicism economically and temperamentally impossible in these islands, but he gave into the hands of a ruler of real force, Parliament, an instrument that Oliver so signally failed to wield. Oliver, however, was a sentimental, a picturesque figure ; Thomas, a cold scientist, acting according to the maxims of Macchiavelli, the writer on government who was the most critical in his attitude that the day had yet seen arise.

Thomas Cromwell, indeed, gave us Modern England. He gave the country not only the blessings it enjoys, but also its chief problem. He destroyed Catholicism and the rule of the noble ; he gave us Protestantism and a democratic instrument that is as nearly perfect as any that has yet been known, since, from the days of Cromwell's modification of Parliament, it has very effectually registered the will of the people at such times as the people was in the frame of mind to have desires or to pay attention to public matters. On the other hand, when the people has been lethargic, Parliament has never failed to bow to the will of strong individual rulers, such as the Tudors or Sir Robert Walpole. Yet Cromwell had no passions and no humanitarianism. To the modern ideal, that the State is great where individuals are happy, he would have answered that where individuals are happy, the State is strong, and is so constituted as to suit the needs of strong individuals. Because this latter part of his doctrine was not carried out, because humanitarianism came creeping in, our modern

State is defective; we have compromised, as we are perpetually compromising. And the result is a perpetual discord, a discord that we have never muddled through into any harmonious resolution. It was the Redeemer who first said that the poor are always with us, who first glorified the poor, who first adumbrated the vision of a State adapted to the needs of the weak and of the humble. But Cromwell was more than anything an opponent of Christ, or was more than anything indifferent to Christianism. In a rough and ready way the Church, before the sweeping away of the monasteries, attempted to mould states into the forms of Christian Commonwealth. The Church took the poor under its protection. It attempted to wrest from temporal powers as great a portion of their resources as it could. It administered more or less wastefully these resources, using them primarily in the interests of the cult, and secondarily in those of the poor, who are God's brothers. Thus after a fashion they left for Cæsar as little as they could of the thing that was Cæsar's, and rendered all the rest to God. Mediævalists, some humanitarians, idealists, and others, seeing the immense body of poor men that the great monasteries supported, see also in this arrangement the ideal charity, the ideal method of disposing of those poor who are always with us. And indeed, the ideal is a fine one. But it should not be forgotten that Cromwell also had his panacea for the poor—a panacea perfectly simple, perfectly direct, perfectly logical. This was the rope.

Cromwell desired to render unto Cæsar—unto a State infinitely strong—all the things in the world. God might have the rest, nor for the poor either was there any place in this republic. Under his auspices the rope was used unsparingly ; in thousands and thousands, as rats come out of a demolished haystack, the poor came out of monastery after monastery that Cromwell demolished ; and in thousands and thousands, under the auspices of the Flail of the Monks, the poor were hanged. This was the logical consequence, this was the inevitable result of a strong, of a Christless State. And it is only because our rulers since then have wavered between statecraft and mercy that we have with us still the great problem of the modern State. Wealth varies in relation to the population and humanitarianism in relation to wealth. Thus it is significant that humanitarianism, as exemplified in Socialistic ideals, had its birth during the period, one of the very few periods in the world's history when means of production had overtaken the birth-rate. Thus whereas Socialism in England during the Victorian period was, under the auspices of men like William Morris, of a purely idealistic nature, Socialism to-day is of a nature scientifically economic, tempered, as must always be the case in England, with humanitarian sentimentalism.

True Toryism and true Socialism have been pointed out to amount in the end to the same thing. Both aim at the establishment of a strong State made up of efficient individuals. But whereas the new

OBJECTION TO THE CRITICAL ATTITUDE

Socialism is still tempered by such watchwords as Fraternity and Equality, the old Toryism was in any humanitarian sense utterly remorseless in its dealing with the weak. And it is probable that the death of the old Toryism and the dislike that is felt for the newer forms of Socialism, are alike due to what is logical in their ideals. And it is equally probable that as the Socialistic ideal develops, so it must become more and more logically remorseless in its dealings with humanity. At present its aims are limited to knocking off the idle rich; but these once disposed of, it will perforce turn its attention to the non-productive poor. Idleness is a disease, misfortune is a disease, poverty is a disease, and the healthy State cannot afford to contain diseased members. That advanced thought will eventually have to deal with such diseased members upon lines similar to that of Cromwell with his rope, we need not very much doubt. If Socialism get the upper hand, its tendency will be towards the equal distribution of wealth. But with population and the taste for luxuries—the necessity for luxuries—increasing day by day, however equally wealth may be distributed, eventually there will come a time when the production of the world will be insufficient to meet the necessities of its peoples. As soon as that juncture arrives— and it may be said that that juncture has already arrived—the necessity for dealing stringently with the non-productive will become imperative. It is incredible that any statesman to-day should venture to say that the unhealthy shall by law be prohibited from breeding. It would probably be impossible even to introduce any such Bill into the House of Commons. Yet, some such law rigidly enforced would go very far towards solving the social problem. At present, not only does the State suffer degenerate persons to multiply, but by every means in its power it keeps alive the degenerate products of such unions, and in innumerable ways supports colonies of unnumbered creatures, maimed by mental and physical diseases.

For all of these in the modern State the only logical remedies would be starvation, the axe, or the lethal chamber. Civilisation has no time to deal with the criminal or the diseased in any form. As to whether the criminal exists there may be two opinions, so that there may be two opinions as to how he should be dealt with. But that, logically speaking, the consumptive or the sufferer from any permanent infectious disease, or the man or woman who is temperamentally unlucky, or who, let us say, through drink habitually commits mean actions—that these degenerates should be either executed or relegated to pest colonies as in mediæval times the lepers were—that this is the logical corollary of the modern commercial state, no thinking person could very well deny. But imagine the dislike that would be felt even by the normal, the prosperous, and the perfectly healthy for the constructive critic who first seriously enunciated this doctrine, or for the statesman who attempted to enforce a Poor Law based upon it.

OBJECTION TO THE CRITICAL ATTITUDE

For the fact is, that logic is unhuman and that criticism, though it need not be actively inhumane, must, as far as possible, put aside sympathy with human weaknesses. All men, all books, all projects, and all methods of art must have the defects of their qualities. And it is the duty of the critic to point out these defects as well as these qualities. If it be granted, to resume our illustration, that a Poor Law system based on kindness will be a drag upon a State whose necessity is economic strength, it would become the duty of the critic of that State to put forward some such theories as those we have uttered in the last few pages. It would become his duty to put these theories so strongly, so remorselessly, and so convincingly, that he would secure a certain modicum of attention. Now, supposing that the ordinary, kind-hearted man should become half convinced that the good of the State demands the annihilation of the unemployed, that in fact he cannot have at one and the same time a sound State and more mouths to fill than food to fill them with, this ordinary, kindly man will feel pain. Deep in his heart, deep in the hearts of all men lies the belief that we can eat our cakes and have them; that we can make omelets without breaking eggs; that in some way mysteriously, whilst august and inscrutable Destiny for a moment averts its glance, effect will dodge cause. We desire that our preachers shall give us comfort in the night by preaching through the day these comfortable doctrines; we desire that our statesmen shall find means to enrich the poor without impoverishing the rich ; we desire that new standards shall be set up without damage to old traditions— or we desire as a last resort that these things, if they have to be done, should in no way be brought to our attention.

We should like, that is to say, to see an Act passed that would exclude all aliens from these shores, and that we should be able at the same time still to proclaim that England is the home of liberty, the succouring-ground of all that have fallen in lost causes, the asylum of all oppressed peoples. Thus we pass an Act which ensures that no alien shall land unless he have in his pocket a certain sum of money, or travel with a first-class ticket. In that way we imagine that we may distinguish the sheep from the goats, and that Kosciusko with fifteen pounds in his pocket, or Garibaldi travelling saloon, may be sifted from M. Cartouche, who has stolen forty thousand pounds' worth of jewellery, and from M. Alphonse, whose traffic in human flesh gives him a princely revenue.

The critic is the person who points out that such results will not spring from such enactments, and that is why the critical attitude is so detested.

ON THE FUNCTIONS OF
THE ARTS IN THE REPUBLIC

CHAPTER II

ON THE FUNCTIONS OF THE ARTS IN THE REPUBLIC

I

IT is customary to consider that the State—the republic—has among its functions the fostering of two kinds of things affecting the welfare of the body politic. These it is customary to call the higher things—which are mysterious and connected with the soul—and other things which, if they had never been called the lower, are materialistic, and affect the welfare of the body. In our own country, as we shall have occasion to point out, the State limits itself almost entirely to temporal matters. It is true that we have a State Educational System, but one that, except in its very lowest branches, is so inefficiently designed as to have very little relation even to the material need of the country. To the moral or intellectual improvement of the race, State education conduces very little or almost not at all. Instruction, as it is given in our Board Schools, is probably the best in the world—though it is as well to keep this fact a secret, lest the ratepayer clamour that this instruction must be made less efficient, so

25

that a half-penny in the pound may be taken off his rates. But, whatever merits the system of primary instruction in these islands may have, education, which is a thing very different—the purpose of which is to broaden the mind and not to fill the mind with facts—education of this sort is not provided by the State at all. And, properly considered, one of the chief, if not the chief purposes or moral values, is to give a sense of what life is really like. For this, the English State in no way provides, and for it all the provision that is made is made by various corporations or individuals more or less in competition, more or less in rivalry one with another. And, because of this rivalry, because of this competition, such forces as seek to be educational must become vitiated—the preacher must preach acceptable doctrines, the writer must paint life rosily and in acceptable colours, the painter must render a world all pretty, and all truth must be respectably dressed out.

But the chief value of the arts to the State is that they are concerned with Truth. And if, at present, the arts have very little place in the economy of the nation, it is that they devote themselves comparatively little to the life that we really live. We are existing in the backwash of the Romantic Movement, a movement which, if it gave much pleasure, caused also certain definite evils. For, when every novel had its hero, and every picture its heroic figures, then every man was led to believe himself supported by Providence, the centre of the particular affair with which he was concerned. Such a doctrine may lead to boldness in the presence of dangers ; it may confer good consciences and directness to the glance ; but it takes away fortitude in the time of protracted trial.

It should be remembered that the life we live to-day renders us dependent on the arts for our knowledge of life in a degree that probably never before obtained. We have so many more small contacts with our fellow-men ; we have so much less knowledge of how men really live. So that almost every man of normal life to-day has the greater part of his view of the world from vicarious experience. He has nowhere else to go until it is too late. So that the painter who neglects to see beauty in the things which surround him, the poet who cries that happiness was only to be found in remote fields of distant ages, sin, in their degree, as much against youth as the novelist who, forcing always happy endings to his tales, draws a picture of life too easy and too slack.

For, if the arts have any functions at all, that function is truly educational — nay, it is truly scientific. The artist to-day is the only man who is concerned with the values of life ; he is the only man who, in a world grown very complicated through the limitless freedom of expression for all creeds and all moralities, can place before us how those creeds work out when applied to human contacts, and to what goal of human happiness those moralities will

lead us. In times when speech was less free, this
was different. When the rough and ready attractive
qualities of a Tom Jones were a passport to the great
majority of human hearts, a man able to model
himself on that free hero was fairly certain of success
in life, since the greater portion of humanity would
look kindly on him, and would smooth his path.
Or, in the days of Albert the Good, a man who
modelled himself on the heroic figures drawn by
Mr Smiles might very easily scrape together anything
from a modest competence to a large fortune, and he
might attain to a perfect tranquillity of conscience
and a sure hope of heaven by practising virtues of
a simply commercial kind, in imitation of George
Stevenson, of Brindley, or of Thomas Edwards. But,
nowadays, life is slightly less happy-go-lucky than
it was in the eighteenth century. It is slightly less
commercial than it was in the days of the Prince
Consort, and it is much more bewildered than it has
ever been since the Dark Ages. As we shall have
occasion to see later on, so many small things crave
for our attention that it has become almost impossible
to see any pattern in the carpet. We may contemplate life steadily enough to-day : it is impossible to
see it whole.

So that it is only in the pages of naturalistic novels
that we can hope nowadays to get any experience
of modern life, save that individual and personal
experience of our own which comes always too late.
The methods of grubbing up wealth, which obtained

FUNCTIONS OF ARTS IN THE REPUBLIC

in the days of Mr Smiles, are, by now, if not absolutely
ineffectual, at least—in face of the great trusts, of the
great stores, of the great " combines "—to all intents
and purposes obsolescent. And, if we are no longer so
tranquilly confident that there is a heaven to get
into, we are at least perfectly certain that a flaccid
and self-satisfied commercialism is not the only way
to obtain to a sure and certain hope of the blessed
resurrection. So that it is in the hope of discovering
whether there exists in these islands any trace of a
sober, sincere, conscientious, and scientific body of
artists, crystallising, as it were, modern life in its
several aspects, that these pages have been written.
And, for the matter of that, it was for the definite
and unashamed purpose of promoting such a school,
were it found to exist, or did it seem possible to
found one—it was for this definite and unashamed
purpose that the *English Review* was begun. For,
if what we have said above be granted to be true—
that life is a thing so complicated that only in the
mirror of the arts can we have a crystallised view
or any vicarious experience at all—if this be granted,
it must follow that only from the arts can any safety
for the future of the State be found.

Nothing was more true than the words of Flaubert,
when he said that, if France had read his " Education Sentimentale," she would have been spared the
horrors of the Franco-Prussian War. For, during
the period before 1870, France had drifted for a time
into the same happy-go-lucky frame of mind that

29

has always existed in England. And so exactly did Flaubert depict this frame of mind in this his most monumental book, that could France have set itself seriously to the task of reading and pondering upon it, undoubtedly some tightening up of the national character must have taken place. France, however, amiably ignored the masterpiece, just as, in all probability, England would ignore a similar work did it produce one. It is perhaps none of our business to prophesy national disaster. The British tradition of muddling through has worked well enough in the past : may it work so in the future. It is an open question whether literature is ever an influence—whether it is ever more than just a symptom. On the one hand, Don Quixote may have swept away the last traces of chivalry from the world ; on the other, it may have been merely a symptom that chivalry had exhausted its usefulness. But, inasmuch as it remains a possibility that the arts can mould a national character, we may seek to welcome such of the arts as appear likely to be beneficial : we may well welcome them even if they are only a symptom. For, being only a symptom, they would bear witness to the fact that, in at least part of the nation—and that part the most vocal and the most influential—there was working a certain leaven, a leaven of courage, of seriousnesss, and of sincerity. And the arising of such a school, putting forth a quantity of work sufficiently great to influence influential minds, would become an historical event of capital importance.

FUNCTIONS OF ARTS IN THE REPUBLIC

That it would be commercially unsuccessful is to be premised and to be neglected. But that it should exist, this school, this bulk of work, is the first necessity of the State, for it would be the symptom of national health.

Indeed, the appearance of any great body of imaginative effort, the work of authors singleminded in the effort to express, and felicitous and successful in expressing, in imaginative terms, all that is most real, most permanent or most fugitive in the life around us—the appearance of such a great body of imaginative effort would have to be regarded as an event at least as important in the history of a civilisation as the recording of the will of a sovereign people with regard to some policy of exclusion, of admission, of humanitarianism, of pugnacity. For the record of events, assimilated by the human mind to-day, moulds the event of to-morrow, and the nearer the record comes to registering the truth, and to so rendering it as to make it assimilable by the human apprehension, the more near it comes to being an historical expression, the more near it comes to being an historic event itself.

Speaking broadly, literature at the present day divides itself into two sharply defined classes—the imaginative and the " factual "—and there is a third type, the merely inventive, which, if it be not in any way to be contemned, has functions in the republic nearly negligible. The functions of inventive literature are to divert, to delight, to tickle, to

31

promote appetites ; of imaginative literature, to record life in terms of the author—to stimulate thought. By this, we do not mean to contemn the faculty of invention, a faculty which, in the history of English Literature, has been all too wholly contemned. The power to tell a story is as essential to the artist as is, in human affairs, the body to the soul ; and the common superstition of the English writer that to take any old story—the history of the fall of Troy, that of the Prodigal Son, or an episode from Richard of Gloucester's chronicles—and to use it as if it were the framework round which to mould a sculptor's fabric of poeticised atmospheres and studies of character, this singular Anglican heresy is probably as much as anything responsible for the extremely small hold which imaginative literature to-day has upon the body of the English people. It may indeed be said that, in certain forms of art, a work of imagination without invention is almost as nugatory as a work of invention without imagination. That perhaps is an exaggerated statement of the case, but it is for the moment worth setting down.

It is a statement worth setting down, because, exaggerated as it is, it may awaken thought, and the province of the imaginative writer is by exaggeration due to his particular character—by characteristic exaggeration, in fact—precisely to awaken thought. That is to say, that this is his utilitarian function in the republic : his actual and first desire must be always the expression of himself—the expression of himself exactly as he is, not as he would like other people to think him, the expression of his view of life as it is, not as he would like it to be.

It is for this reason that the work of a really fine renderer of the life of his day is of such great value to the Republic. For whatever his private views may be, we have no means of knowing them. He himself will never appear, he will never buttonhole us, he will never moralise. He may be a Republican, he may be an Anglican ; he may be a believer in autocracy. But he will never, by the fifth of an inch, drag round his pictures of life so as to make it appear that, if the social state were what he desires it to be, all would be well with the world. We shall rise from extremely protracted readings of his works with the feeling that we have assisted at a great number of affairs, of having met a great number of people whom we should just recognise.

This is the true characteristic of modern life, in which intimacies are so rare, in which social contacts are so innumerable, in which it is no longer a matter of long letters, but of the shortest notes. And what we so very much need to-day is a picture of the life we live. It is only the imaginative writer who can supply this, because no collection of facts, and no tabulation of figures, can give us any sense of proportion. In England, the country of Accepted Ideas, the novelist who is intent merely to register—to *constater*—is almost unknown. Yet it is England probably that most needs him, for England, less than any of the nations, knows where it stands, or to what it tends.

II

'But, if certain writers might—and certain writers do—in a splendid aloofness, present these tenuous aspects of modern life, there is another aspect of work which is called " fiction." In this, it may convey the subtlest speculations of metaphysical or the most *doctrinaire* of social philosophies. It is obvious that the author, being the creator of his characters, may, if he will, create himself. So long as he creates his own character so as to be interesting and to fit into the scheme of the work, he may let this portion of himself preach whatever doctrines he desires. In his own pages he may stroll in and out amongst the figures, he may moralise upon their actions ; he may, by his own actions, modify their psychological workings. The only limit to this form of propagandising is set by the interest of the reader, the only restriction upon the author-character is that of his own conscience. If he act indeed as a *deus ex machina* solving all problems set by the story, then the book must be regarded as a mere Utopia. But if the author, regarding himself as benevolent but meddlesome, fine yet malicious, generous but naturally unsound (or even supposing he psychologise himself as a villain, if he represent himself as marring fine destinies and making evil fortunes), then indeed this propagandist author will be giving us a rendering of modern life as exact as could be desired. He will be attempting to give us the world as he sees it—a world interesting to the measure of his personal value. He too, will *constater*, not colour, the life of which he treats.

It is, however, to the drama rather than to the novel, that we must go for examples of this particular form of rendering of life. It would perhaps be too daring at this juncture to say that the play of " Hamlet " reproduces intimately the story of Dr Socrate, or that Mr Barrie's professor, of " The Professor's Love Story," very exactly resembles M. Bergeret. Yet, upon the whole, it is to the theatre of Mr Barrie and Mr Shaw that we must go to find the only forms of Art which England has to show as an off-set to the works of the author of " Crainquebille." Mr Barrie is nearly always with us, shedding his gentle, his touching or fantastic beams, but Mr Shaw for too long has coruscated only in the remoter planetary regions. Mr Barrie is generally " running " at the Duke of York's. Mr Shaw, as a rule, may be seen only in the provinces.

Indeed, a person from another world, seeking to estimate the level of intellectual appreciation in England to-day, if he should go as we ourselves do, almost nightly, to what are called " places of entertainment " in London, would be overwhelmed by the fact that, in this proud, wealthy and materially polished civilisation, there was visible—outside the theatres that produced the works of the two writers we have named—no trace, no scintilla, no shadow of a trace of the desire to have any kind of thought awakened. It is true that a few theatres sometimes present us with sinister forms of morality but as much might be said for the Ballet at the Empire, where Mr Farren, by robbing a drunken tramp, escapes magnificently from the consequences of a former theft, and shows us, in a dance shared by Miss Beatrice Collier, an expression of passion that might very fitly be styled a true lyric.

Indeed, it is to the music-halls that we must go nowadays, for any form of pulse-stirring—for any form of any consummate expression of Art. That any man, who is at all a man of the world, could go to a theatre, except on very unusual and uncommercial occasions, is not only grotesque but unthinkable ; that he should go to a music-hall may be lamentable, but it is at least to be understood. For the programme at almost every music-hall in London contains at least one " turn " that is worth considering in moments of idleness. Thus, at the Empire, some such dance as that to which we have referred will repay you for sitting some time in a stall, and one little Cossack dance of Mdlle. Kyasht may be worth another twenty minutes. And, even at the outlying halls—at the Shoreditch Empire itself, for instance—it is pleasant to be amongst simple people who enjoy themselves, and the reception accorded to various performers will cast lights, sinister, tragic, depressing or inspiriting, but lurid enough, upon the circumstances and psychology of the very poor.

This would be the common-sense view of the man of the world ; but we are not saying that we applaud this state of things ; we are merely recording an aspect sufficiently lamentable. Many circumstances contribute to bring this about. Thus, it is obvious that all our first-class theatres are too large for any subtlety of acting. Except from the front row of the stalls, it is impossible to observe the facial play of any actor who does not grossly over-act. This, of itself, debars any rendering of modern life from the stage, for English social contacts of to-day are a matter of repressed emotions. We do not, that is to say, violently contort our countenances when we conduct our illicit love affairs, hear that our banks have failed, or that our wives have been picking pockets. We do hear all these things, but we do them sitting down, with expressions of languor, or with such minute starts and inflections of the voice that they would be totally invisible and inaudible from the amphitheatre of almost any modern theatre. It is impossible. in fact, to represent upon the stage of to-day any English man or woman of gentle or of middle-class origin.

But, perhaps, realism and the drama have, at most periods of the world's history, been entirely at variance. It is certain that neither Mr Barrie nor Mr Shaw come with any frequency at all near to the life we live to-day. Regarded philosophically, each of Mr Shaw's plays resolves itself into a variety entertainment in which character after character does his brilliant verbal " turn " and then retires into the background. It would be too extreme to say that this is the sole characteristic of Mr Barrie, for his chief, his distinguishing note, is the tenderness the justness, of his sentimentality.

And sentimentality is as legitimate a medium as are realism, pessimism or cynicism. The first business of the author is to interest ; his instrument wherewith he interests us is his exaggeration. If that be true to himself, if he be an artist of sufficient attraction, it will convince us of the reality of the story that he tells. Subtlety of speech is impossible upon the stage, for you cannot turn back the leaf to read the speech before the last, and whilst you are reflecting upon the hidden meaning of one speech, you will miss the significance of three more. For subtlety, Mr Barrie substitutes quaintness and appeals to the emotions. For subtlety, Mr Shaw substitutes half-truths in startling aspects. How Mr Shaw would come off, if it were considered bad taste to laugh in theatres, so that speech after speech was uttered without the break and the pause for the inevitable Shavian laughter, we hardly dare speculate. But, whereas Mr Barrie for the time being convinces us, Mr Shaw hardly ever does this. His speakers over-speak, his actors overact, and we are delighted. But a touch of realism will disturb our delight.

This was curiously illustrated the other day at

the performance of " Arms and the Man " at a suburban theatre. Here Mr Barker's Bluntschli of the first act and Miss Auriol Lee's Raina throughout the play were very much more realistic than those of the performers in the cast at the Savoy—very much more realistic, but how much less convincing! Mr Barker was begrimed and panted like a man who really had been pursued by Balkan irregular troops. The consequence was that the *aplomb* of his philosophy of war became almost entirely incredible, for it is human nature to believe that a man who cannot get his breath will not be able to collect his thoughts, whereas we may believe that a man who has just emerged from a paperchase " off " need not be extremely out of breath.

But both Mr Shaw, who gives us real speeches producing an effective unreality, and Mr Barrie, who gives speeches in one evening more sentimental than any collection of real characters could utter in the course of a year—who convinces us, in fact, by very unreal means—both Mr Shaw and Mr Barrie do render some service to the Republic. The one quickens our emotions, the other our thoughts. And it is possible that the drama cannot do more than this, for are not to think and to feel the converse of necessary qualities of a proper man ?

THE CRITICAL ATTITUDE

III

To determine what may be the influence of music upon national character is a task as difficult as to discover which ever came first—the first hen or the first egg. The problem indeed is almost exactly the same. The elementary musics of Scandinavia, of Scotland, and to a less extent, of France, are profoundly influenced by the fact that their earliest national instrument was the bagpipe.

The plaintive character of Scottish melodies or of such melodies as the old French fishermen's song is due almost entirely to the fact that they were sung to the accompaniment of a drone and, in certain instances, to the fact that, in one form of pipe, the chanter lacks a note of the diatonic scale. Other races first evolved the stringed instrument, plucked by a finger or a plectrum. This gives to the music of Spain, of South America, of the American negro and—according to Mr Kipling—of the Englishman overseas, its peculiar rhythm and peculiar power to excite certain emotions.

A Scotch melody will make you mournful, a negro melody will fill you with the desire to dance, but it would be a daring man who would say that the Scotsman is mournful because his chanter lacks the leading note of the scale and that the buck negro struts and cakewalks because his first instrument was a gourd across which was stretched a sinew of some beast. On the other hand, the profound modification which

FUNCTIONS OF ARTS IN THE REPUBLIC

is taking place in English popular—as opposed to English professional—music must, one would imagine, produce some change in the English national character, or, at any rate, the character of that part of England which is urban.

The history of English music is an exceedingly sad one. You have to remember that, until the coming of the Hanoverian sovereigns England made a music of its own—a music tender, poetic, sweet and fresh as is the English landscape. Before the Reformation, England had a race of Church composers as solemn, as noble, as emotionally religious and as scientific as any that the world has produced. These, however, or such of them as existed in the days of Elizabeth, fled to Rome—they were mostly church or cathedral organists—and in the Vatican their masses and anthems are still hidden. Such few anthems of theirs as remain, we have still with travestied words in songs like " The Leather Bottel " or " The Vicar of Bray."

The Church composers being gone, there remained a group of musicians of whom the name of Lawes may be said to be typical. These culminated in the splendid, the supreme genius of Purcell. For, as Shakespeare stands to England, so does this great poet of sounds. That he is forgotten, that he is never performed, that his beautiful melodies remain as hidden as do small and delicate pink shells beneath the ocean's sands—for this we have to thank George II. and Mynheer Handel.

THE CRITICAL ATTITUDE

In those days, there came in the professional musician, so that now, in a barber's shop, we find a halfpenny paper. In the time of Charles II. in similar establishments, there hung upon the walls lutes and viols and when four or five customers were gathered together, they were accustomed to beguile their waiting with what was called a " consort " ; for a man who could not add extempore another part to a ground bass was considered to be no gentleman. From the time of Handel onwards, the man who could do this received that negative title. " Fiddler " we imagine is still a term of contempt. At this day, we may see the very same process operating on a small scale in the north of England.

In Yorkshire and in Lancashire, there has been since time immemorial a population largely made up of practising amateur musicians, moorland bands, choral societies and the like, all excellent performers, producing, scientifically and beautifully, excellent music. But, as happened in the south of England two centuries ago, so in the north nowadays the professional musician is depriving the amateur of the desire to do anything more than form an audience. With his excellent means of transit and his cheap places of entertainment, the Yorkshire miner and the Lancashire cotton-operator go, instead of three nights a week to their band or glee-singing rehearsals —to the music-hall. This is perhaps lamentable ; it is, at any rate, inevitable.

FUNCTIONS OF ARTS IN THE REPUBLIC

But, if in the north, the music-hall is destroying the practice of music, it is, the optimist might think, doing in the south something to redress the balance. For there can be no doubt that the popular song of to-day, with its more elaborate harmonies, its more characteristic rhythms and its occasionally real rendering of feeling is at least an expression of something like the emotional life of the people. Such a song as " Champagne Charlie " or as " Two Lovely Black Eyes " was an expression of mere imbecility, whereas some which we hear to-day are at least expressions of passion. And what is most curious in the popular song of to-day is its pronounced negro colouring.

A large percentage of the songs sung by the most popular performers at the music-halls has the peculiar rhythm, the peculiar full-close and the peculiar long, high notes that may be heard in the cane-brakes and the corn-fields every evening. And the odd mixture of the precise and formal cockney dialect with the negro musical mode evokes, from audiences of the proletariat, enthusiasms which, if they do not seem incredible to us at least do us good to hear. In the meanwhile, separated by a deep chasm from really national life, the " concerts " of the professional musicians continue. They continue, these performers, as it were, in another sphere, like angels playing upon celestial instruments, remote indeed from any national necessities. The trouble with the professional concert consists, of course, in the professional. On him or her so much more interest is centred than on the art he dominates. And, in his multitude, what with the exigencies of advertisement, of charity performances, of the sheer difficulty of securing a hearing he himself is having what is called " a bad time."

Indeed, the position of music is very much that of Literature. We all, who attend concerts, are on the look-out for a rising star. Some of us believe that this will come from Russia, some from the Near East, some from France, some from Germany. With the death of Brahms, the race of great figures amongst composers seemed to come to an end. If, however, we desired to afford prognostications, we should say that, probably, from France, which in its music retains its haunting characteristics, possibly from the United States negro, or by a very remote chance, from these Islands, a new, sweet and great music might arise.

Probably it would arise, if, as seems likely, the professional executant should be starved out of existence. The immense troops of foreigners who have followed Handel would then come no more, and music productions being out of the hands of aliens, the English public, with its natural craving for music, would be forced itself to satisfy its own desires. It might then be possible to form—which it certainly is not now—a quartette party in any provincial town, and we might go on to that ideal state, when a grand piano, a flute, a violin and 'cello should be found in every barber's shop. And this might cause to arise from the midst of a multitude of amateur composers, some thousands of composers who would seriously train themselves, and some few Purcells. This indeed might seem the vision of a madman—of a bemused alienophobe—were it not that, two hundred years or less ago, this was actually the case with the music of England. That it was so, you have only to go to the pages of Mr Pepys to prove. Did he not write a song called "Beauty Retire," and did he not expect his wife's maids to sing his song, and join a consort when it was necessary? And was not even the Puritan Colonel Hutchinson, that high soul of the gentlest birth and breeding— was he not "an incomparable fingerer of the lute?"

IV

Since the Plastic Arts are, in this country at least, most recognised by the State, we may, in their case, more definitely than in those of their sisters, trace their effects upon the people as a whole. For we are concerned with the people as a whole; with the body politic, not with classes cultured or productively artistic. For Music, the State and the Corporations do very little : for Literature, nothing at all is done —of a State expenditure of £160,000,000 per annum, £400 is paid for the production and fostering of Letters. It is paid to the Poet Laureate : we believe indeed that it is paid to him, not *quâ* poet, but in his capacity of Historiographer Royal. But upon

THE CRITICAL ATTITUDE

architects, sculptors and painters some sums of money are spent year by year—not perhaps enough to pay in any one year for a torpedo-boat, but still some money. What then does the State receive in return?

What actually can the State receive in return for its services to the Arts? Immediately, certain financial benefits. By its beauty, a city may attract visitors : by its monuments, its paintings, its dramatic performances, its operas. It would be difficult to estimate how many people the purchase of, say, the Rokeby Velasquez attracts to London. But let us make, tentatively, the essay. We are personally acquainted with two German gentlemen, with one Frenchman and with one Italian, who have made visits to this country with the single purpose of studying this masterpiece. Let us say that the National Gallery contains one hundred masterpieces, each of which attracts four specialists per annum. Let us put their expenditure at £10 each per visit. Thus, from the class of strict specialists alone, we may set it down, tentatively, that the National Gallery attracts £4,000 per annum. Let us say that the attractions of the Tate and Wallace Galleries are half as valuable, those of the South Kensington and the British Museums of equal value. We arrive at a working hypothesis that, from the student class alone, the National Collections draw a sum of £16,000 per annum. At £4 per cent., this represents a capital value of £400,000.

Let us add to these, say, ten times as many people

46

who come attracted to the National Collections as a whole, and we arrive at a capital value of £4,000,000. Let us add again ten times as many as this last class on account of another class who visit this country, not so much for the purpose of seeing its monuments and its Art treasures, but to whom the existence of these things is the determining inducement for a visit—the intelligent Chinaman, Japanese or Hindu, who wishes to " do " Europe for the sake of social prestige, or because his ladies desire to " shop." We arrive thus at a capital value of £40,000,000. And this is in addition to the actual value in the market of the works of art themselves. We think, therefore, that we have proved to the intelligent business men who conduct our affairs that money spent upon the Arts is not only money invested in sound securities, but that it adds distinctly to the good-will of the nation as a going concern.

In fact, it should be the ideal of a State directed upon soundly commercial lines to become the Art centre of the world. It pays. Indeed, nothing pays so well. London is the largest city in the world, largely because she is also the pleasantest, and she is the pleasantest almost entirely because of her gentle and delicate æsthetic appearance, on account of her grey days, her grey vistas that so admirably soften and harmonise her masses of architecture.

To the cultivated reader, these sentiments may appear merely ironical or merely paradoxical, but, actually, they are sound and dry sense. The attractiveness, the " pull " of a city, consists in innumerable small magnetisms. In the first place, it must be accessible, and perhaps it is only finally that it should turn its attention to the task of being attractive. This it may do. This it will most surely do by paying attention to the Arts. It is, of course, impossible that London should be the literary centre of the world, although the English language is that most widely spoken and most widely written. But there is an inherent individualism in the English man of letters : there is an inherent shame in him, which makes him desire to be regarded as anything but a man of letters. His aspiration is to be always a social figure, a philanthropist, a preacher, a fisherman, or a " man of action." The actual practice of his craft thus loses its cohesive force, so that it is almost impossible to find in England what is found in almost every other European capital—a society of men eagerly discussing their Art, sinking personal jealousies in the thirst for mutual sharpening of the wits, in the divine curiosity to discover how things are done. The Englishman of letters of any distinction lives apart, dotted over the face of the country, each one isolated, as it were, upon a little hill. He has no Academy like that of the Immortal Forty ; [1] he belongs to no movement, and in consequence, the Art of Letters in England has practically no social weight and practically no contact with the life of the people. The English public takes some, but very little, interest

---

[1] I do not say that there are *no* academics.

in the Art of Letters. The English man of letters takes none at all. The English State devotes ·00000025 of its expenditure to this, the most despised of the Arts, yet, when we consider how much the election of a new Academician in France adds to the gaiety of the nation, when we consider the canvassings, the discussions, how much the city stands on tip-toe and what a distinguished function the delivering of the discourses creates, we see that the Art of Letters, by its mere machinery, adds immensely to the attractiveness of the City of Paris. And there are all the other academies and societies — societies of " admirers of M. Verhaeren," of " admirers of M. Saint-Paul le Roux the Magnificent " –scores of societies, all these adding to the social amenities, the gaieties, adding to the " pull " of the City of Paris.

We have, we believe, one such society in England, but it is devoted to the practitioner of a sister-art. And indeed the case of the other Arts in England is very different. We have musical festivals. We have an expensive Opera. We have Royal Academies of Music and of Painting. The Royal Academy of Arts, if it be a body falling lamentably short of any high ideal of the fostering of the Arts, and if its commercial tactics be of the most ludicrous description yet, whatever its shortcomings, the Royal Academy exists. It has a certain power of attraction. Its private views are functions conferring some social distinction on the Fine Arts. Its exhibitions attract

D
49

large numbers of not very intelligent people. Still
it exists, and it attracts, and occasionally its exhibitions, contain, carefully skied, or hung to as much
disadvantage as possible, works that are almost
works of genius.

Now, if the State, realising the commercial
advantage of the Arts to the nation, instead of
delegating benevolently its functions to the purely
commercial gentlemen who form the Royal Academy
of Arts, could open its eyes to the extent of seeing
that it would be really profitable to pay attention
to two things, we might put the Empire upon a very
safe commercial basis, by insuring against national
calamities. For money spent in adding æsthetic
amenities is the best of all insurances for a nation.
It is, of course, a good thing to build battleships.
To frame tariffs may or may not be profitable. It
is possible to contemplate the hypothesis that trade
will follow a flag. But flags, in the inevitable course
of years, are trampled in the mud. The time arrives
for all nations when, trade being gone, all tariffs are
useless. And eventually, all battleships end on
the scrapheap or on the sea-ooze. Then a nation that
has its Parthenon or its Sistine Madonna finds its
account.

Moreover, there is the influence of the Arts upon
national character. Italy is Italy, not only because
it contains Siena, Rimini and the Pitti Palace. It
contains the lovable Italians—the men whom generations of æsthetic traditions have rendered lovable.

FUNCTIONS OF ARTS IN THE REPUBLIC

That anything would ever render the Englishman lovable, or induce the English State to aspire to the building of a Parthenon—that may seem an aspiration to an unthinkable perfection. But, by pointing out —by proving—that it would pay, we may have done something. We may never have a Parthenon : perhaps, one day, we may nerve ourselves, say, to the extent of being proud of the National Gallery, or of cleaning out from that Augean stable, the Tate, its huge proportion of dreary and inane canvases.

ENGLISH LITERATURE OF TO-DAY.—I

CHAPTER III

ENGLISH LITERATURE OF TO-DAY.—I

WE have set ourselves the task of determining for the uninstructed reader the difference between the writer of the commercial book and the writer of a book which shall be a work of art. When it comes to results this is a matter of great difficulty, demanding of the analyst a cool faculty of criticism, a broad catholicity and great powers of self-abnegation in the realms of taste. Suppose, for instance, we consider the case of a debatable writer—let us say George Eliot. Here was an authoress almost omnipotent in her power to charm at once the great multitude and the austere critic of her time. She was taken more seriously than any writer of to-day ever has been, or ever will be taken. Yet, to the great bulk of educated criticism of to-day, George Eliot has become a writer unreadable in herself and negligible as a critical illustration. Her character-drawing appears to be singularly wooden : her books without any form, her style entirely pedestrian and her solemnity intolerable. And it is probable that it was this very solemnity that gave to her works all the qualities that make

them to men in touch with the life of to-day so entirely
unreadable, so exactly like so many heavy cakes.
George Eliot was, in fact, a great figure. She was
great enough to impose herself upon her day ; she
probably never sought, though she certainly found,
the popularity of sensationalism. Taking herself
with an enormous seriousness, she dilated upon sin
and its results, and so found the easy success of the
popular preacher who deals in horrors. She desired
that is to say, to be an influence : she cared in her
heart very little whether or no she would be considered an artist.

Let us place her alongside another writer of her
day whose ambition did not soar above producing
a good " household article." As an artist—as a
mere writer—Anthony Trollope had most of the
vices of George Eliot. He is never remarkably
engrossing, his writing has no particular justness of
phrase, his novels are hardly constructed at all, but
meander one into another without any particular
bounds, without there being any particular reason why
any given book should begin or end here or there.
Yet, although Trollope's books do not very much
cry aloud to be read, we can take up with interest
" Barchester Towers " in a hand from which nerve-
lessly " Adam Bede " drops. The reason is that
never taking himself with any attempt at solemnity,
Trollope was content to observe and to record, whereas George Eliot, as if she had converted herself into
another Frankenstein, went on evolving obedient

monsters who had no particular relation to the life of her time—monsters who seduced or admitted themselves to be seduced, who murdered their infants or quoted the Scriptures just as it suited the creator of their ordered world. Trollope, on the other hand, observed the world he lived in : his characters walk upon the ground ; perhaps they are even a little flat-footed, but his observations have the light of facts, filtered through the screen of a personality. That the personality was not a very rare, was not a very subtle one, is perhaps the reason why we do not read him with very great avidity. But because the personality, was so honest so humble and above all, so conscientious, he helps us to live in a real world, he affords us real experiences. And precisely because George Eliot had no conscience, precisely because she gives us a world that never was, peopled by supermen who, we may thank God, never could have been, she is now a moral force practically extinct, is hourly losing impetus. And she has as an artist no existence whatever. Having studied " Das Leben Jesu," she became inflated by the idea of the writer as prophet, she evolved monstrous works which contained her endless comments upon Victorian philosophy, forgetting that our Lord, Who was the supreme influence, because He was the supreme artist, limited Himself in His recorded fiction to the barest statement of fact, to the merest citation of instance.

Having stated so much we may pause to concede that probably the great majority of humanity would

THE CRITICAL ATTITUDE

say that the converse of what we have stated is the actual fact. They would say, precisely, that George Eliot was the great artist because she presented them with an unreal, with an idealised world, which is what they demand of art. George Eliot, that is to say, takes them out of themselves. Mr Trollope makes them think. With this, of course, we cannot quarrel, since it is merely a matter of terms. We prefer, that is to say, to consider that the artist is the renderer of human vicissitude—the creator of a world of his own in which conscientiously, as he sees it, effect follows cause. We should not, supposing each of them to render life as he saw it, quarrel with Fielding, whose idea of cause and effect is that drinking makes a man a fine genial fellow any more than with the late M. Zola, who wrote a book called " L'Assommoir." Actually " Tom Jones," since it is a more filtered work—since it is the product of the author's experience of life, whereas Zola's book is a product not of experience, but of tabulations—" Tom Jones " will probably have a more persistent vitality. It is a rendering of life ; it is, such as it is, a picture of manners. It interests because it excites our curiosity. After all, we most of us read because we want to know—because we want to know so many things. We want to know how people used to live in past days, we want to know what happened to a given character ; we want to know what was the outcome of a given affair. We want to be, as a Stevensonian writer would put it " at grips with life."

ENGLISH LITERATURE OF TO-DAY

That there are innumerable methods of attaining to this end is nothing to the point, and it is nothing to the point to say that the greatest works deviate occasionally from the strict sequence of cause and effect. Thus the plots of Shakespeare are the evolutions of an infantile mind—the merest followings out of the more foolish parts of folklore. But we do not read Shakespeare for his plots, we read him for his texture, for his personality, for his charm. And whilst making these concessions to his genius we are apt to forget that he would have been an even greater writer if he had more frequently lapsed into the sense of the realities. " As You Like It " is a great comedy, but it would be infinitely greater did it not end in a farrago of childish impossibilities. And Shakespeare, if he had taken time to think upon these matters, would have been as great an artist as Tourgénieff. He would have remained none the less great a poet.

We may, indeed, see in the condition of the Stage to-day a rather ominous, a rather terrible warning as to what in the present circumstances Literature in England is coming to. At the present moment the Literary Art is almost entirely confined to the novel. In a literary sense the " serious book " hardly exists at all. It is, for instance, almost impossible to name any historical work of late years that has any educational, as opposed to an instructional, weight : it is difficult to name any work of a social or political nature that has any literary value. Historical works are nowadays assemblages of facts presented in an utter baldness of manner. Works social or political limit themselves to bald statements of doctrine supported by such tabulations and statistics as suit the purpose of the writer. The "memoir" of to-day is a loosely strung necklace of anecdotes without, as a rule, any attempt to give a view of the subject's personality or to render the atmosphere of the world in which he lived. It panders, in fact, almost wholly to that love of " ana " —of tit-bits—which has always been the distinguishing feature of the English reader.

Ruskin, Carlyle, the late Mr Gladstone, Fred. Archer, Colonel Burnaby, Sir Frederic Leighton, the late Duke of Edinburgh, Sir Charles Russell, Sir Frank Lockwood and the late Colonel North—the fact that all these people once spoke or did not speak to the subject of the memoir : a remarkable shot at a markhor, a dinner at the Savage Club with a catalogue of the guests present, some maudlin regrets for the passing of an extinct music-hall, some lamentations that Sir Henry Irving is equalled by no actor of to-day—all these things shaken together and written down without any particular regard for sequence or for any of the unities—there you have your book of memoirs of to-day. That the public appreciates this fare every publisher knows quite well—the average book of memoirs sells, indeed, better than the average novel. It is, in consequence, a better speculation, and simply because it does not appear under the guise of fiction it is regarded as a more respectable venture. But that any page of any book of memoirs published now will remain in the minds of any of their innumerable readers we are very much inclined to doubt. That the reading can, and will, profit nobody we are very certain.

The downfall of the seriously historic book has come about because the writing of such works has fallen into the hands of the schoolmaster—into the hands of the specialist. And the aim of the schoolmaster—of the professor—becomes inevitably not education —which teaches the marshalling and the analysis of facts—but instruction which teaches merely their collection. The historic book of to-day exactly shadows the attitude of the modern University towards history. There is no particular attempt to awaken an historic sense, but enormous efforts to secure a meticulous knowledge of a small period are encouraged. An average historic curriculum for one of our Universities would prescribe to-day the acquiring of a very loose acquaintance with five hundred years of English history, a study more serious of some particular century, a study *au fond* of some fifty years and then a study, minute beyond belief, of five to ten years of that fifty. And the candidate will be given to understand that he cannot, by any means, expect to attain honours in his subject unless his examiners be afforded proof that he has done what is called " original work "—that is to say, the candidate must bring forward some new documents, some new statistics or some new measurements of battlefields. Given the purpose of the educational bodies of to-day we need have no particular quarrel with this system. But it is obvious that it is a system calculated to turn out, not educated men who will write great books, but specialists who will go on discovering documents. And, inasmuch as what emoluments and honours there are will go to those who have distinguished themselves in such academic courses, the commissioning of historic books will fall almost altogether into the hands of these specialists.

The compiling of histories is to-day put into the hands of committees of such academic historians, each writer being allotted a period as to which, with the sanction of his University, he is considered to be an authority. And thus we have such a phenomenon as a late volume in a very respectable historic series. Here the writer was allotted a given century as to which he was considered to be the best authority. Some seventy years of the hundred he treated per-functorily as being of no significance. He permitted himself occasional inaccuracies, which would have been trifling in a historian merely literary, but which are much less pardonable in a work of reference. He omitted to attach any particular weight to the financial policy of the chief Minister of that period—a financial policy which changed the whole course of English affairs. In revenge he devoted by far the greater portion of the book to a minute analysis of the events of some twenty years of the century. He produced, in fact, an elaborated version of such a paper as would entitle a University candidate to honours in history.

We are not, of course, inclined to quarrel with this tendency. The production of works of reference is a laudable occupation. But the fact remains that at the present day these works of reference have stifled any literary activity within the domain of history. And the tendency has bred an almost worse evil—it has led to the production of innumerable works concerning themselves with the secret lovers of queens, with king's mistresses and with the debaucheries of the favourites of the various decadent sovereigns that the world has seen. This is a class of book which again, though the profits far exceed those of any conscientious novelist, is detrimental, not so much because it panders to the baser sexualities of the idle—indeed, hardly any of these volumes are produced with sufficient skill in portraying an atmosphere to pander to any passions at all—but because they combine with the daily press and with the popular memoirs to which we have alluded in affording the mental anodynes with which the English reader of to-day so persistently drugs himself.

The characteristic of modern life that is most appalling is its inability to sustain any protracted train of thought. Thought consists in the classification of matter, in the perception of analogies, and, as a subsidiary branch, in the arriving at an exact means of expression. And in this sense thought is as much discouraged by, is as distasteful to, the scientific historian as it is to the hack-writer who assembles salacious details. The province of Art, however, is the bringing of humanity into contact, person with person. The artist is, as it were, the eternal mental prostitute who stands in the market-place crying : " Come into contact with my thought with my visions, with the sweet sounds that I cause to arise—with my personality." He deals, that is to say. not in facts and his value is in his temperament. The assembler of facts needs not temperament at all but industry. He does not suggest, he states, and save in the mind of professed thinkers, he arouses no thought at all. But the business of the artist is to awaken thought in the unthinking. Tolstoi has said that the writer should aim at interesting the agricultural labourer alone, and the dictum, if it be exaggerated after the manner of this considerable rhapsodist, is nevertheless an exaggeration of great value. What it means technically is that the artist should strive to be explicit. What it amounts to in practice is that the artist should consider himself as writing for the uninstructed man *bonæ voluntatis*— for the absolutely uninstructed man who is of his own type. And the more men there are who are of his own type, the greater will his appeal be, the greater his sympathies, the greater the effect of his art upon the world.

To this wideness of appeal, to this largeness of sympathy, the specialist can never hope to attain.

He addresses himself to an aristocracy, since he addresses himself to the instructed. The province of Art is to appeal to, to solace, the humble. The excuse for the existence of the artist is that he voices the unvocal of his own type. He has no other claim to dominance : he has no other right to the six foot of his country's ground that he will finally claim. The specialist exists and has the right, drudge-like, to exist to the measure of the industry that God has vouchsafed to him : the compilers of salacious memoirs and of contemporary reminiscences, the writer even of commercial fiction and of the negligible drama, have a right to exist which they share with the licensed victualler. They supply drams to the brains of men too weary to think and too much caught up in the machine to feel.

We have been celebrating recently the bi-centenary of Dr Johnson, the greatest, because the most representative, of all English figures. That he was the greatest of all English writers outside the realm of imaginative literature, we should hesitate categorically to set down, whatever our private tastes might lead us to feel. But the point is that for a writer such as Johnson there would be to-day no chance of existence. He is unthinkable. If we look upon the " serious book " as it is produced to-day, we see that there is no room for clear, for logical, for merciless thought, and such an essay as Johnson's upon Shakespeare if it so much as found the light of day, would be received with a chorus of sentimental outpourings of indignation.

THE CRITICAL ATTITUDE

Johnson, of course, was no particular hand at the compilation of facts ; he was before all others the thinker who rendered the verdict of common sense upon any given set of facts. No such writer is to-day required. We have no critics but we have panegyrists, we have no desire to face remorseless thoughts, though we are pleased occasionally with those quaint paradoxes that are half truths. Froude and Carlyle were bad enough in their day, but they had at least the courage to seek to find a pattern in the carpet. And if Carlyle's " French Republic " or Froude's " Henry the Eighth " are, historically considered, of little value compared with the work of the scientific historian of to-day, they have at least the merit of bringing us into contact with their authors—with men who were human beings, who were fallible but vital, who were childish, but upon occasion Titanic. And this is the especial value of the art of writing to the reader of to-day. The world is so full of a number of things, facts so innumerably beset us, that the gatherer of facts is relatively of very little value. And when, each man by himself, we are seeking to make out the pattern of the bewildering carpet that modern life is, it matters very little whether the facts are those collected by the scientific historian, by the sociopolitical economist or by the collector of railroad statistics. But to be brought really into contact with our fellow men, to become intimately acquainted with the lives of those around us, this is a thing which grows daily more difficult in the complexities of modern life. This, vicariously, the artist is more and more needed to supply. For, as we have formerly remarked, the tendency of humanity is to crowd into the large cities, and within their bounds to live semi-migratory lives. Of the history and of the thought of the great number of men with whom we come into contact we have no knowledge at all. We see them for the allotted minutes, for the allotted hours. Of their lives and passions we know nothing. So that unless the imaginative writer help us in this matter we are in great danger of losing alike human knowledge and human sympathy.

We will delay, for the moment, our dealing with the modern novel, but there remains a much older Art, that of the Drama, which may claim our immediate attention. The condition of the Drama in England is a matter of interest for the student of Literature. By those of the critics who are most impatiently modern we are told that the Drama is at its very lowest ebb. By those old enough to remember the Robertsonian days, the view is held that the Drama is upon the up-grade. And probably the latter is the case. Struggling very fiercely against the necessities of commercialism—and the Theatre more than any of the other Arts is under the grip of finance—there has been arising on the English Stage a small tendency to bring the Drama into some contract with the life that we live, and to instil into the actor some sense that his is a profession with its dignities, its call for self-sacrifice, its decencies.

THE CRITICAL ATTITUDE

Commercialism must always have its grip upon the throat of the London Theatre. Rents are very high, rates are very high, lighting is very costly, and advertising is only obtained at the cost of a system at least as expensive as that of ordinary blackmail. The price of seats, therefore, is also unreasonable and the manager has evolved the theory—in which at first sight the public would appear to back him—that the public must have something for its money. And the something takes the form of elaborate scenery of, unreasonably costly pageants and of childish stage-realism. These things must necessarily be the death of Literature upon the Stage. For, for Romeo to describe in impassioned terms the moonlight, when an excellent representation of the moon is shining in the face of the audience is the merest tautology. And it is absurd for a lover to chant the beauties of his mistress when the audience can see her. They can judge for themselves of an actress's personal charms. Similarly all verse, fine writing and even impassioned speeches must strike false notes upon a stage realistically set.

The truth of this was very readily to be seen at the Haymarket when Mr Herbert Trench's Repertory Company produced " King Lear " in a setting beautifully inspired by the late æsthetic movement and extraordinarily realistic in all its atmospheric effects. The end of all similar ventures is that from any point of view of a harmonious representation the production is an entire disappointment. So long as any action is in progress the play holds the attention, but the moment it comes to speculative or descriptive passages in the text, the moment it comes to any monologue at all, the effect is one of disappointment and of ennui. To hear Lear describing the storm in the appalling din produced by sham elements, to have to strain one's ears to catch his voice is to lose all the pleasure in the matchless verbiage, whereas, to have heard Mr Norman M'Kinnel, who played Lear, reciting these passages upon an ordinary platform in every-day dress would be to feel with the feelings of Lear and to see and hear inwardly all the pitilessness of the storm. Shakespeare, in fact, has given us scenery, atmosphere and human emotions. All that the stage-manager has to provide for him is declamation. Anything more that he provides spoils Shakespeare's effect. For it should be remembered that in a modern sense Shakespeare was not a playwright; he was a poet who wrote novels for recitation. And any attempt to revive the Shakespearean literary play upon the modern stage is doomed simply to failure, since it is inspired by a want of knowledge of the materials in which the playwright works. No scenery, however skilfully painted, can appear absolutely real to an audience, and the actor, if he succeeds in holding attention, does so not with the aid, but in spite of his surroundings. At the Haymarket, for instance, it was very difficult to enter into the spirit of Kent's monologue in the stocks since people do not soliloquise in such situations in real life, and since

THE CRITICAL ATTITUDE

Mr France need only have reached out his hand to undo the thirlpin and set himself free.

We confess, therefore, that the production of the Repertory Theatre filled us with disappointment. We had hoped that Mr Trench would have given us renderings of Shakespeare more in consonance with the poet's art. The one great advantage of a really Shakespearean production of one of Shakespeare's or of any literary play would be its relatively small cost. This would mean that many more trials could be made. For the great cost of modern theatrical productions does harm to the art of the Drama, not only by the false realism of its settings but also because it kills speculation. When a manager must put all his eggs in one basket he becomes—as we had occasion to say of the modern publisher—exceedingly timorous as to what that basket shall be. He cannot afford to put plays on for trials. In consequence the infusion of new blood into the ranks of dramatic authors is a matter of an extreme slowness. And the production of any play with any newness of situation, of handling, or of point of view, becomes increasingly difficult. Nevertheless, the Drama—even the purely commercial drama—seems to move more and more into contact with the life of the people. If the reader will take the trouble to consider the annexed plot of a play which aims at being no more than an agreeable evening's entertainment, he will see that, in spite of certain absurdities which are apparently inevitable to modern conventions, there is some attempt at the handling of an idea and the solution of a problem :

" Two married couples have joined in taking a cottage in the Island of Mull for the fishing. The husband of the one and the wife of the other amuse themselves by having a flirtation, which sets up intense jealousy on the part of the remaining husband. The bereft wife thinks of the value of a sense of humour in these circumstances and persuades husband No. 2 to pretend to be violently in love with her. This works extremely well in the case of Sir W. Hutton, but Viola sees through their game and instead of herself becoming jealous she simply plays up to them. Here we have the ground for many farcical incidents, one of the choicest being the butler's espionage and delight in the prospect of appearing in the witness-box of the Divorce Court in a red tie and a fancy waistcoat." [1]

Or here again is the analysis of a plot by a dramatist of a more considerable skill, standing and aspiration : [2]

" This is a play well-handled and carefully executed, but the characters are all the obviously stock ones. The question it raises is whether the making of a gentleman of the present day is a thing to be desired for the race of the future. The beginnings of all gentlemen must have been very similar, and even after having been gentlemen for several generations

[1] " A Sense of Humour."   By Beryl and Cosmo Hamilton.
[2] " The Making of a Gentleman."   By Alfred Sutro.

it is doubtful whether one in like circumstances would or could have acted differently from Mr Sutro's. But we think that Mr Sutro has no serious social object in view ; he means simply to amuse and to show us his skill in handling puppets. His gentleman, Mr Archibald Carey, was made by pickles, Harrow and Oxford, and when twenty-six, practically a beggar, he finds that he is as incompetent and as unwilling to earn his livelihood as a gentleman not made by pickles. He is an easily influenced young man. After whole-heartedly offering to go and make some pickles with his father, he takes his sister's advice and finds it more to his liking to mend his fortunes by marrying a rich widow, one close to hand, one possible to be fallen in love with quite sincerely within four hours' time. The father is a well-drawn character of a self-made man founded upon the Père Goriot of Balzac."

So that with Sir Arthur Pinero producing at the St James's his usual play, we have the usual drama of commerce at its usual height. In the meantime Sir Herbert Beerbohm Tree at His Majesty's presents us with a Spectacle, which in a dim way is an advance upon most of the spectacles that he has hitherto given us.

Of the three dramatists that we have mentioned, Sir Arthur is the best equipped technically. But although he selects excellent subjects and treats them in the most spirited manner imaginable, squeezing the last drop of effect out of each situation and building the whole up to the most effective imaginable crisis, so steely hard is his temperament, so entirely wanting is he in any quality of heart that his characters fail, not only in exciting sympathy but even in interesting us. Mr Sutro, on the other hand, whilst distinctly below Sir Arthur Pinero in technical achievement has about him a considerable touch of humanity. His figures are largely stock figures, but he does attempt to sympathise with them in their worries, or to use the larger word, their problems.

The province and the powers of the Stage are so enormous because it speaks to the public in the crowd. It has an appeal which no book can ever have, simply because the book must always speak to units. A crowd is quickly swayed, emotion running from individual to individual cumulatively until an enthusiasm is raised such as only elsewhere is caused by orators and preachers. For this reason the play is a much coarser form of art than that of the writer of books. And if its effects upon the crowd are swifter, so they go less deep. The Drama, moreover, is a very interesting thermometer of the state of public desires and necessities, for the public, if it is affected by the piper, to a very great extent has the privilege of calling the tune. Thus in the great mass of printed literature that is purchased to-day there is no very particular tendency since there is at the present moment no very overpowering national desire, no very overpowering national necessity, no visible public danger, nor any all-embracing enthusiasm. For this reason books on social and political subjects have no marked type, have no particular appeal and fall under no particular classifications. And in the case of novels no classification whatever is possible. Comparatively speaking a writer writes a book to please himself, and comparatively speaking a playwright writes a play that will appeal to his audience. His work being purely temporary he attempts to make as much as possible of the dominant interest of the moment.

The Drama of the day is frequently condemned because it deals almost exclusively with matters of individual contact—it deals with divorce, with sexual attractions—with the problems, that is to say, of how people may live together at home, and not with the great subjects of History, Political Economy, Public Morals and the like. But if we regard with an unprejudiced eye the state of civilisation to which we have attained, we shall see that this is its almost logical outcome. The province of civilisation is so to instruct or so to coerce bodies of men that they shall live together if not at peace at least without much friction. And in the present stage in England, as far as the outside of our houses is concerned, we have arrived at a fairly considerable pitch of civilisation. Household lives at peace with household, the Roman Catholic and the Baptist dwell side by side without any burning desire to employ the faggot or the rope. Tory no longer attempts to shoot Whig in public places. Whig no longer attempts to attainder

Tory. And if at all Class is arrayed against Class, its weapons are the taxes to be imposed and the ballot-box which infers the power to impose taxes. And these conditions hardly afford much material for handling by the dramatist. (We shall consider later the cases of Messrs Granville Barker, Galsworthy and Bernard Shaw.) For the Drama, painting everything with a broad brush and being the essentially popular art that it is in modern conditions, must have incident to keep it going, and in the more public and broader aspects of life, incident is to-day a thing so rare that it would outpass the probabilities to include in any one Drama a sufficiency of incident to keep the ball rolling.

The problem then of the English Drama of to-day is not as to how people of differing creeds, nationalities and customs shall steal fragments of the world one from another, but as to how people may best live together in the same household. A great many years ago a dramatist called Ibsen wrote a play called " A Lady from the Sea." Here the problem stated was how one of a married couple should retain the other in her domestic fidelities and duties in face of the illicit, the adventurous and the alluring. The end was obtained by giving the departing partner her " head." No sooner was she told she might go with the mysterious and blue-eyed stranger than the wife suddenly discovered that romance had gone out of the situation. She returned to become an excellent spouse, a fond mother. This possible solution of

domestic duties was received at the time with jeers
by the English public. Two years ago, however,
Mr Barrie produced "What Every Woman Knows."
Here the problem was the same and the same the
solution. Having perhaps reflected upon Ibsen's
Drama, or seduced by the more winning qualities
and the quaintnesses of Mr Barrie's views, the public
at any rate in the crowd in the theatre accepted Mr
Barrie's panacea for domestic ills. Soon afterwards
Mr Somerset Maugham produced his play called
" Penelope." Here again the problem stated was
exactly the same. An erring husband desired to pass
his time with an attractive lady not his wife. He is
permitted to do so, he is encouraged to do so to his
heart's desire. As a result he tires of the extraneous
attractions and returns to his domestic hearth. And
if the reader will consider the plot of Messrs Beryl and
Cosmo Hamilton's play, he will see that these authors,
attacking the same problem, deduce from it the same
result in a play of negligible value intended to appeal
to the least thinking class of audience. Thus this
idea filtering down from the harsh utterances of an
austere playwright who at his most popular was
appreciated only by a small intellectual oligarchy in
England—this idea has descended through the tender
quaintnesses of Mr Barrie, through the comparative
frivolities of Mr Maugham, writing in his more popular
vein. It has become a stage property, it has become
one of the texts from which the dramatist can preach.
It means, that at any rate in the homes that are

reached by the Drama, a nodding acquaintance has been m.. e with the idea that it is best to ride the domestic horse with a loose rein, with a light hand. Sir Arthur Pinero, it may also be observed, handles the problem of domestic relations whilst Mr Sutro considers the problem of social contacts. So that if in the Drama of to-day there is little subtlety the dramatist has come to realise that in order to interest his public he has to preach from texts concerned with the public's interests. It would have been inconceivable that any of the plays we have alluded to could have been produced in Robertsonian days. Sir Arthur Pinero has travelled immensely far in the direction of rendering modern life as it is since he wrote " Sweet Lavender." The Mr Barrie who wrote " What Every Woman Knows " is a Mr Barrie much more earnest than the author of " The Professor's Love Story." Even Sir Herbert Beerbohm Tree saw fit, a year or so ago, to give us as his autumn attraction a piece of spectacular atheism, a glorified version of Mr Shaw's " Showing up of Blanco Posnet." And these are only the plays of commerce.

In them, it is arguable, we may see that the commercial drama, poor and unsubtle as it is, is on a higher basis as far as problems of modern life are concerned, than are the commercial novel, the commercial history, the commercial memoir and the commercial socio-political work. For any particular poetry, for any particular originality of outlook, for any particular human sympathy we look to this class of Drama in vain. But it has in some cases a certain seriousness, in other cases a certain pretence of seriousness, that are encouraging to find in any of the more popular forms of the art of writing.

ENGLISH LITERATURE
OF TO-DAY.—II

CHAPTER IV

ENGLISH LITERATURE OF TO-DAY.—II

O F non-commercial English dramatists three names at least are worthy of consideration. They are those of Mr Granville Barker, Mr John Galsworthy and Mr Bernard Shaw. These writers we may call non-commercial because sincerely, according to their abilities, they adhere for their stories, their " plots," to the probabilities of life in the particular plane of life in which they elect to deal. They avoid, as far as they can, the meretricious coincidences of the conventional stage, the screens, telephones, melodramatic discoveries by injured husbands and all the rest. They attempt to present us with really human figures caught in the toils of vicissitudes really human, acting as human beings really would do in a world such as these Dramatists, each after his kind, may chance to see it. This is most particularly true of Mr Granville Barker and least so of Mr Bernard Shaw. The attraction of Mr Shaw is that of unreasonable brilliancy. The sallies of his characters hold our attentions but they do not engage our sympathies. We are delighted with his figures whilst they talk, but all the while we are subconsciously aware that we do not believe that any group of human beings so ready with their tongues ever existed. The consequence is that Mr Shaw's plays—and it is with this purpose that he sets out to write—may very well awaken thought. But it is as to the ideas expressed by his characters rather than as to their human and personal problems that we are set thinking. The idea which is aroused in us by the conclusion of " Arms and the Man " is that an hotel-keeper may possess as many table-cloths, horses, servants and opportunities for hospitality as the owner of Arundel Castle. This may or may not be a fruitful jumping-off place for a train of thought. But we are not interested as to whether the Swiss mercenary and the daughter of a semi-savage will make a good match of it. We are not interested in their fates, because neither Captain Bluentchli nor Raina are very much more human than two talking-machines uttering witticisms of the familiar timbre of Mr Bernard Shaw. And just because ideas as to ideas are relatively valueless in comparison with the ideas aroused by human problems, so the effect of Mr Shaw's work is comparatively transitory. Not one of his plays will leave as much mark upon the emotions as, let us say, " The Playboy of the Western World," by Mr Synge, now so untimely dead. Mr Synge's play was not realistic in the sense that it was a parcel of life obtained by striking an average of the daily papers. It had, however, that deeper realism which comes with sincerity and with human sympathy

It had the realism of the fairy-tale and when we looked at the " Playboy " we said, " By the Grace of God there might go ourselves." For the " Playboy " has the adventurous spirit which is in all of us—that adventurous spirit under whose afflatus poor humanity continues to strive against all the odds, hoping, as it were, to bluff Providence and to stand at last a triumphant hero upon some stage.

Of the more commonly accepted form of realism Mr Barker's work, and more particularly his " Voysey Inheritance," is the best example that we have. Mr Barker's actual output has been so small, his activities in other fields have been so multifarious and so exhausting, that he must be regarded as a figure rather of promise than of achievement. But all his work has the quality of making us believe that when we have witnessed it we have been present at an " affair." It is as if we watched from our windows several people walking along the street and were told : " That man is So-and-so ; he desires such and such things. That man is Mr ' B.' His bank balance is exceedingly overdrawn. That lady is Mrs ' C.' She permits Mr ' B.' to manage her investments and they are all going to the house of Mrs ' D.' a widow who has accepted a proposal from Mr So-and-so, but would prefer to elope with either Mr ' B.' or her chauffeur." And in witnessing Mr Barker's plays we have, as far as his stories are concerned, some of the engrossment that comes from listening to gossip about people whom we see and know, and added to it the satisfaction of knowing that the gossip is true. In the texture of his dialogue Mr Barker has nothing of Mr Shaw's brilliancy. His characters, as a rule, are rather dull normal people. That they seem to be people who have all of them read Mr Shaw's works does not detract from their reality. So many people have read Mr Shaw's works. But just because his dialogue is not so brilliant, Mr Barker's characters are more real stuff of life. They talk, it is true, like inverted Nonconformist ministers, but their talk does not influence their actions in the least. Thus it is in real life. This characteristic was singularly evident in Mr Barker's story, "Georgiana." Here, though the characters talked with the ponderous gravity of members of Ethical Societies, their actions, which it is true took place only after a tremendous amount of talk, were precisely those of any other couple determined to achieve an illicit entanglement. And this again, is life : it is as much what every man does as "The Playboy of the Western World" was what every man desires to be. Thus to us Mr Barker appears the most promising of present-day dramatists.

Mr J. M. Barrie is much more difficult to classify. His works have achieved such immense popularity that in the strongest sense of the word they are commercial successes. But Mr Barrie impresses us— we are not of course talking of his personality—as a figure that has wandered into, that has never sought, commercial success. He appears a little bewildered, a little timid, a little like a modest and unknown man who walks on to a platform of an immense gathering to find himself in the most unexpected manner overwhelmed with plaudits. And perhaps what Mr Barrie has found is not so much commercial sucess as universal affection. He handles his themes with such timidity that every now and then he arrives sincerely at something which very much resembles the stage device of the commercial dramatist. In " What Every Woman Knows " he adumbrated a problem of an extreme seriousness ; he played round it in his charming manner until the very last word of the very last act. And the very last word of the very last act evaded the problem—with a little joke. That this is exactly what the public wanted is Mr Barrie's good or bad fortune, but, that Mr Barrie wrote that little joke because he thought the public would want it, we are sufficiently certain was not the case. He wrote it because all that was timid, gentle and charming in his unassuming soul as a writer wanted that little joke. It expresses its author's yearning to see life as an affair in which little jokes will not only count but solve problems : it is the product of a child-like mind seeking to see in a very complicated world a quaint, a trixy fairyland. And just because the make-believes of a child have about them nothing that is repulsive, Mr Barrie's artificialities do not inspire us with dislike. If there is about them nothing very courageous, there is about them also nothing that is mean. It is not Mr Barrie's province to be a prophet. It is his place—and how excellently he fills it !—to satisfy that side of human nature that craves after quaintness. If he does not ask us to look a grim world in the face he hangs up before us a gauze curtain through which we see dark valleys and level masses of tree-tops and the stars sparkling artificially. The little lights shine out in the trees, the windows of a little hut light up and the witch sails away on a broomstick.

How considerable a literary skill Mr Barrie had whilst he still wrote novels is to be seen by any one who will take the trouble to read " A Window in Thrums " or " Auld Licht Idylls." These for their workmanship are almost the most attractive that we have. For workmanship—for getting an effect with the fewest number of words—Mr Barrie was almost the equal of Mr W. W. Jacobs to-day and of Mr Kipling in his early years. And that his attention to methods of producing an effect in pure Literature aided him very materially when he came to attack the Drama we need have very little doubt. Some doubt we may have, for the technical qualities required to conduce to excellence in the Drama are almost entirely the converse of those called for in the production of written Literature. It is seldom sufficiently re-membered that the difference between the play and the novel is identical with the difference between the spoken speech and the printed page—the differ-ence between Rhetoric and Literature. Rendered enthusiastic or rendered sympathetic by the tones and gestures of the actor the audience will pass, will applaud, sentiments and situations which upon the printed page, time being allowed for reflection, would appear gross, absurd or vapid. One of the most considerable preoccupations of the novel-writer is to give his characters personality, form and voice. One of the most attractive of the resources that he has at his disposal is the rendering of atmosphere, of the appearance of natural objects and the utterance of thoughts not immediately appreciable by hurried minds. For the dramatist, as we have already pointed out, none of these resources are permissible. Nevertheless, to hold an audience a play demands a greater degree of technical skill than any other form of imaginative writing. For in the end the province of technical skill is simply to interest. And speaking very roughly the quality in an Art which interests us is the quality of surprise. The small quaintnesses of Mr Barrie hold our attention for this reason, and for this reason, the plays of Mr Galsworthy—another considerable dramatic author whose early training was in the novel—hold our attention. And this is more particularly true of Mr Galsworthy than any other of our novelists. It is probably the reason why his plays are more satisfactory than his novels, why, as a dramatist, he is in the first rank, whereas as a novelist his place is much lower.

For, if the dramatist must be more sedulous perpetually to interest his audience, so he works in a coarser material. His effects must be more obvious since an audience has no time to reflect ; his surprises must be such as the mind can grasp immediately. In the novel, as in the play, Mr Galsworthy pursues the quality of surprise with a dogged, an unblinking persistency. You never catch him nodding ; he never nods. But whereas it is the province of the really great novelist to conceal his æsthetic methods —by which means he achieves the appearance or the actuality of subtleness—the dramatist has no need to make this one step further in the realm of Art. He must, indeed, stop short of subtlety. This Mr Galsworthy just does in his novels as in his plays.

We have amongst us, at the present time, perhaps some six purely imaginative writers whose work it may be here profitable to study in the effort to discover whether there exists any school of conscious Literary Art in England to-day. For ostensibly there is nothing but a formless welter of books without any tendency as without any traditions or æsthetic aims. Of these six writers three—Mr Henry James, Mr Joseph Conrad and Mr George Moore—we may regard as being wholly concerned with their Art, as belonging to the School which represents the mainstream of the current of European Literature, and as having nc external considerations for anything but their individual presentations of life. We have Mr Galsworthy, whom we may regard as belonging technically to the same school, but as falling short of ultimate preoccupation with his Art. And we have two imaginative writers who, not artists in the strict sense that they have any canons of Art by which they work, yet by virtue of personalities attractive or unusual, carry on in the typically English manner the traditions of the insularly English novel. These are Mr H. G. Wells and Mr Rudyard Kipling. These writers do not, of course, exhaust the catalogue of novelists whose work is worthy of attention or perusal, but they stand out as very excellent sign-posts to mark the difference between the more insular and amateur and the more cosmopolitan and scientific schools of writers at present at work in these kingdoms.

Mr Conrad and Mr James stand so far above any other imaginative writers of to-day, that their signific-ance and their importance are apt to be a little lost. They stand, moreover, so far apart one from another that they have, as far as any literary movement is concerned, an entire want of unity or cohesion. They are united by one thing—by an extreme literary conscientiousness. With personalities so absolutely differing that the fact is obscured, the literary methods of each are in essentials the same. Each takes in hand an " affair "—a parcel of life, that is to say, in which several human beings are involved—and each having taken hold never loosens his grip until all that can possibly be extracted from the human situa-tion is squeezed out. The defect of each as an artist is his too close engrossment in the affair he has in hand. In each case this leads to what is called digressions. Mr James digresses because he desires to build up round his figures an immense atmosphere of the complexities of relationships. He loses hold, from time to time, of the faculty of selection ; he will step aside to introduce some subtlety of relationship because it is quaint or because it amuses him ; he will neglect to observe that this subtlety does not help his story forward and that thus he has gone outside his mainstream. Mr Conrad is much less concerned with spiritual relationships and much more with a sort of material fatalism. For him every one of the situations of a book must be rendered inevitable. The actual situations thus set up he is less careful to define. In that way he is an impressionist. If he had to describe, let us say, a murder, he would give his story the true tragic note. The motive for the murder would be overwhelming, the circumstances in which it was brought about would be so described that we should imagine ourselves to be present at the actual time. But not only this, Mr Conrad would find it necessary to describe minutely the knife with which the murder was committed, the manner in which it fitted into the murderer's hand. Nay, more ; supposing the murderer to be an individual of a wild or an excited appearance, Mr Conrad's conscience would make it necessary that he should minutely describe the man who sold the murderer the knife. He might provide us with the genealogy of the seller in order to prove that owing to the idiosyncrasies of his father and mother he was predisposed to the selling of lethal instruments to men of wild appearance. Or he might give us an account of the vendor's financial ups and downs for the preceding two years in order absolutely to convince us that the vendor was inevitably forced by destiny to dispose of the knife. In the former case the cap of the vendor's mother and the photographs over her parlour mantelpiece would be carefully described in order to render *her* real ; in the latter, the knife-seller's account-books would be sedulously projected before us, and at the moment when he was hesitating whether or no to sell the knife there would float before his eyes, written in red ink, the amount of the balance against him at his bank. But these digressions, if they serve to take up time, do give to Mr Conrad's works its extraordinary aspect of reality. Without them we should not feel that we are experiencing—at least to the extent that Mr Conrad would experience them—the actual scenes that he describes for us. Without them, indeed, it is very likely that Mr Conrad's impressionism would fail of its effect. For having minutely described the purchase of the dagger, Mr Conrad would go on to render for us the journey of the murderer in a four-wheeler through a thick fog. We should be conducted to the door of a house where the crime was to be committed, the rust of the knocker would be felt, not seen, because of the thickness of the fog. The door would open upon a black hall and there the episode would end. The point would be that Mr Conrad would by this time so entirely have identified us with the spirit of the expedition that we should take up the tale for ourselves. We should go up the creaking stairs which Mr Conrad beforehand would have described for us with such intimacy that we should feel ourselves simply at home ; we should push open the door and in the shadow of the bed-curtains we should perceive a sleeping form. But Mr Conrad, having dropped his story with the knocker upon the front door, would begin his next chapter with an observation from Inspector Frost, of the Secret Service. He would describe the room in which Inspector Frost sat and he would give us the inspector's biography, with an episode of his school life which would go to prove how inevitable it was that the inspector should pass his days in the detection of crime. And so once more Mr Conrad would take up the story of the murder with the inspector's description in colloquial English of what the corpse's hands looked like.

But it is to be observed that any faults at all cardinal in the writings of these two great artists arise from nothing but their too great attention to their Art. Their defects, in short, are those of overconsciousness. It may be observed that both Mr Conrad and Mr James are somewhat limited in the range of life which they treat. But that again is a form of conscientiousness, since a writer can only really write with assurance of the life which he himself has lived. And it is the characteristic of both these writers—who were trained in the same school— that they are unable to write with any pretended feeling of assurance of the planes of life with which they are unacquainted. They are, that is to say, in the strictest sense, realists, whether they treat of the romantic and the far away or of the everyday and the here.

Both Mr James and Mr Conrad are products of the great French school of writers of the eighties. They are thus in the main-stream of that development of modern Literature which, beginning with Richardson, crossed the Channel to influence Diderot (we are thinking of his " Ramean's Nephew "), and the Encyclopædists, to issue, as it were, by means of Chateaubriand into that wonderful group whose fervour for their Art drew together Flaubert, Maupassant, Turgenev, the Goncourts and the rest. Mr James is, as it were, more essentially the child of Turgenev, Mr Conrad draws his blood more widely from the whole group, but it is safe to say that had these writers not existed, neither Mr James nor Mr Conrad would have written at all as they do. There remains one other very distinguished exponent of this school whom we have left unmentioned—Mr George Moore. Mr Moore once delivered himself of the witticism : " Mr James came to Europe and studied Turgenev. Mr Howells remained in America and studied Mr Henry James." Mr George Moore, on the other hand, left Dublin to study Guy de Maupassant. And so closely has he assimilated the technical methods of the author of " Une Vie " that, except for the language, " Esther Waters " or " Evelyn Innes " have nothing to show that they did

93

not emanate from the pen that wrote " La Maison Tellier." The technical excellencies of Mr Moore are probably unsurpassed in the world at the present time. If he has any rival it is M. Henry de Regnier. In reading " A Drama in Muslin " we experience exactly the same sensation that comes to us in the perusal of, say, " Mariage de Minuit." There is the excellence of description, the hard, cool style, the hard, cool characters and, in the mind of the reader, a lasting hunger for the illuminating phrase. We read on, filled with admiration, we expect the something revelatory until the very last paragraph, until the very last line, until the very last word. And at the very last word there is nothing, no illumination, no suggestion, nothing. The book has ended and that is all. We may put it down in a sort of literary shorthand that both Mr Moore and M. de Regnier are lacking in the gift of poetry. And by the gift of poetry we mean not the power melodiously to arrange words but the power to suggest human values. Mr Conrad and Mr James are both poets because each of their phrases suggests something more than it actually expresses. Mr Moore observes very wonderfully, but in their renderings his observations are frozen. This is probably due to a defect of personality. The face of Mr Moore that seems to look up at us from his pages has cold eyes. He is wonderful but he sets fire to nothing.

Some of this frigidity is present in the work of Mr Galsworthy the novelist : none of it at all in that of Mr Wells, though there is one writer, Mr Arnold Bennett, who, with a view of life singularly similar to that of Mr Wells in his more serious work, has assimilated in everything but style almost as closely to the methods of our great French precursors as Mr James, Mr Conrad, Mr Moore and Mr Galsworthy. Mr Galsworthy's methods as a novelist—whether by accident or design—are precisely those of the Flaubert who wrote " Bouvard et Pécuchet," whereas of the Flaubert who wrote " Cœur Simple " we find in him little or no trace at all.   In his earlier work he was obviously much influenced by Turgenev.   But Turgenev is the great writer that it is the most unprofitable to study for his literary methods alone.   He had, in short, no methods.   He has the most marvellous power of telling a story, the personality of the sweetest poet that there ever was, he has a fine sympathy to bestow upon the oppressed and a fine indignation : he has a sympathy none the less fine for the oppressors.   His methods were his own : his earliest stories are as flawless in form as any that he wrote after he went to Paris.   And having no methods all that the disciple can gain from the study of his work is his point of view.   This, at one time, Mr Galsworthy very faithfully represented.   He radiated, as it were, sweetness and light, but having nothing very particular to say, his work had no special significance.   With " The Island Pharisees," " The Country House," " The Man of Property," Mr Galsworthy entered upon a new stage of his career.   He became, that is to say, the moral observer of the British middle class. And it was then that Mr Galsworthy passed over into the camp of Gustave Flaubert. The whole of British middle-class society became for him, as it were, one tremendous figure of Homais the Pharmacist, of " Madame Bovary." He gives us a British comfortable class of the most entirely unimaginative description and, as was the case with Flaubert of " Bouvard et Pécuchet " his characters vie with each other in exhausting the gamut of imbecilities and of want of intellectual courage. A little later the terrible idea, the terrible phantom of the poor, obsessed Mr Galsworthy's brain. The phase is one through which every social reformer passes or in which every social reformer remains once he has attained to it. Thus Mr Galsworthy is giving us the Literature of agonised materialism. He does not, of course, make the mistake of presenting us with a leisured class uniformly villainous and a poor always deserving. On the contrary, each white imbecility of the rich man is neatly balanced by the black imbecility of the pauper whose toes stick out of holes in his boots. The only difference is that, whilst Mr Galsworthy treats of the comfortable class both objectively and subjectively, when he comes to the poor he treats them objectively alone. This he does, we suppose, under the theory that the poor being so lacking in material matters have nothing but material matters to think of. It would, we imagine, be a mistake to say that Mr Galsworthy takes himself more seriously as a prophet than as a man of letters. But such attention as he pays to social abuses must logically weaken his claim to be considered an artist. And the difference between the commercial writer and the artist is that the latter engrosses himself strictly in his art and thinks of nothing else. The former will, to a greater or a less degree, vitiate the artistic perfection of his book to suit some extraneous end of his own—to gain money, importance, influence or to advocate some cause. He must, of necessity, vitiate his art since art consist in the selection of illustrations. And if we imagine a writer who considers himself born or who grows to consider himself a prophet sent to redeem the State, we shall see how, of necessity, to the extent of his wholeheartedness he will vitiate his work. He will do it with a mathematical precision. The only conscious artists in letters that we have to-day in England belong to the school of Mr Galsworthy. Their method is one of the production of what a barrister would call " cases." They do not obtrude their personalities : they state as well as they can the definite facts of a story, leaving to the reader the task of adopting what moral attitude he will towards a given set of circumstances. This is the modern canon. It will be observed that this elevates the novelist of this school to the rank of a scientific observer. His business is to lay before the reader the results, not of his moral theories, not of his socially constructed ideas, not even of his generous impulses nor even of his imagination, but simply the results of his observations in life. Let us imagine a writer whose passionate theory it was that the great landowner is the most beneficent personality in the State. Let us imagine that this writer, instead of a pamphlet upon the subject, desires to embody his views in a novel. He sets out to discover the best administered large estates. He describes carefully the prosperity of the farmers ; the fertility of the ground. During the course of his novel there will be a cycle of years of fine weather. The kind of seed corn employed will, owing to the investigations of the landowner, be such that more bushels are grown to the acre than anywhere else in the world. We shall be present at a dinner where a beloved land-steward is presented with a silver-gilt punch-bowl by smiling tenants and the happy agricultural labourers will as it were, come out of their rose-clad cottages and beg us to enter and inspect the beautiful water-supply that the Duke has laid on for them. On the other hand, we shall be presented with the miserable case of the small-holder. We shall be introduced to a colony of unsuitable cultivators ; their soil will be of exhausted clay : their landlord will be a corrupt Municipal Council or a cruelly mercenary company working in the disguise of philanthropists. The colony will be situated in the basin of an uncertain river so that from time to time it will be inundated. Their cottages will be always damp, ague will be common amongst them, and since they will have no knowledge either of the methods of cultivation or of how to market their crops, their cabbage plants will fail miserably and they will be swindled by the salesmen in the markets. Now there is nothing to be said against the selection of such a theme. And treated by the large passionately sincere and careless hand of a writer, let us say, of the school of Dickens, the product might be moving in the extreme. It is a theme that, say, Mr Richard Whiteing might handle with profit for himself and pleasure for a great number of readers. Its value as a sociological contribution might be that it would alleviate the lot of a certain number of hard cases. But this theme, if it were treated by a writer with the methods to which we have alluded, would become immediately a much more serious matter. From his restrained methods the reader would gain the idea that the author was treating not of specially hard cases that he had gone out to find, but of what he considered to be the average vicissitudes of modern agricultural life. And with his austere training in a school whose main object is the perfecting of its powers of presentation, this author would convey an impression of austerity and sobriety that would lead the reader to imagine that he was presenting a complete picture of that life. The author, knowing that his business was not to excite the emotions, which is an achievement very transitory in its effects, but to arouse conviction, which is a thing leaving very lasting impressions — the author would be very careful that his exaggerations of fact and motive were each individually very small, each so small as to be individually hardly observable and yet so numerous and so cumulatively persuasive that in the end the reader would be left with a fairly permanent feeling of depression when he came to consider the question of small-holders and with a feeling amounting almost to adoration for the great landowner.

With the sociologically evil effects of such an achievement we are not here concerned. But the point is that such a work, according to the canons of the school which it represented, would be bad art. It would be, as it were, one of the later books of Zola set against, let us say, "Fathers and Children," by Turgenev. Moreover, in a work of art of this particular school constant exaggeration, however slight in one direction, brings in its train the Nemesis of monotony. That, in effect, is why, even for his most enthusiastic readers, Zola's "Rome," "Paris" and "Fécondité" are books lost in a hopeless oblivion, whilst "L'Œuvre" or "Pot-Bouille" remain for them masterpieces.

The fact is that it is a folly for a man to set out upon the task of arousing enthusiasm when his equipment is that of restraint and reserve. The most intellectually influential figure in England at the present day is that of Mr H. G. Wells, and his influence is so enormous because his writings appeal so much to the imagination of the adolescent and of young middle-aged men. Mr Shaw and his colleagues of the Fabian Society have become already the prophets of the middle-aged and of the middle class. To that extent they are upon the wane. Mr Wells' dominion will endure much longer. Outside the circle of those who work consciously at a conscious art Mr Wells is also the most prominent novelist that we have. He has his bad moments and he has his astonishingly good ones. Probably he cannot tell the one from the other. We should imagine that, according to his own views, his semi-scientific stories are of no, or of a merely popular value. Yet, perhaps, his best and most suggestive work of art is " The Invisible Man,"or such a short story as " The Man who could work Miracles." In these, with texts merely negational, Mr Wells is at his ease and comparatively serene. It is only when he becomes constructive that he grows petulant. And this is in the nature of the case, for it is neither difficult to argue nor is it an argument that would cause you much heat, if you are contraverted, to sustain the theory that no man, if he had the powers to work miracles, would profit very much by it. If you so argue, you do not very much care about the facts that you adduce, so that it does not so very much matter if you meet even with stubborn imbecility in your opponent. But the moment you become constructive your theory is an integral part of yourself and you will defend it according to the intensity of its hold upon you until you are worsted in correspondence in the public press or until you have earned the faggot and the halo of martyrdom. It is perhaps foolish—it is certainly perilous for the imaginative writer to attempt to occupy the position of a man of intellect. The imaginative writer, in fact, has practically never any intellectual power whatever except in one or other department of life. His business is to register a truth as he sees it, and no more than Pilate can he, as a rule, see the truth as it is. Moreover, in all intellectual subjects the accepted truth of to-day is the proven lie of to-morrow, and it is only the specialist who can discern in any given realm of human knowledge what is the fashion of to-day and what is permanent. The main energies of the imaginative writer must always be directed to voicing the desires and the aspirations of his day. And this occupying so much of his energies he has not the time that the specialist has at his disposal—he has not the power, the energy or the austerity to state what will be good for to-morrow. This last is in essence the business of the prophet.

So little does Mr Wells fill this rôle that what he prophesied yesterday as being good for himself, for the race, for humanity or for the Solar System, to-morrow he will be engaged upon disproving. When Mr Wells was a biologist he set out to prove—and he proved it beyond the shadow of a doubt—by every muscle in the human body and by every bone of the evolutionally developed higher animals, that a man ought only to have one wife. As a Fabian Mr Wells advocated at least an extension of the Laws of Divorce. What Mr Wells may advocate to-morrow, who but accident shall say ? For Mr Wells is a poet fascinated by the aspects, borne away by the emotions of the moment. He is very blessed and, for the rest of the world, he is very beneficent in that he retains the

heart of a child. His mental career having been one
of adventures and discoveries it is a little difficult at
all shortly to classify him. He writes without the help
of any æsthetic laws, trusting to his personality alone.
The only rule that he observes, as far as we have been
able to discover, is that he never introduces his hero
and heroine together in the first chapter. This is, in
its way, an excellent practice since it ensures for his
novels what musicians would call the sonata form.
Mr Wells is the disciple of no technical school. He
produces a British novel along the lines of his national
temperament. He trusts to his personality, he revels
in it. And, as each new thing interests him, he makes
a book of it. Æsthetically he is the child of artless
writers like Dickens, and by the young men of our
generation he is regarded with an affection as great
as that the whole nation accords to Mr Barrie. A way-
ward person, his writing is at times astonishingly good,
at times astonishingly slipshod. But young Oxford,
young Cambridge, the young men and women of the
medical schools and of the provincial universities
discuss his ideas with the avidity that their forefathers
accorded to Mr Ruskin. To what ends of thought he
will conduct them we have no means of knowing. We
imagine that, supposing him to discover by accident
in an old furniture-shop a piece of Venetian em-
broidery sufficiently beautiful to arouse his enthusiasm
he might end as a Mediævalist. In that case he would
begin to weave beautiful theories as to the Communism
of City Guilds before the thirteenth century and he

would discover once more that life fell hopelessly to pieces at the introduction of machinery.

Mr Wells is, in short, that fascinating and valuable thing, the enthusiast of the moment. He has in Mr Arnold Bennett—at any rate in the Mr Arnold Bennett of the Five Towns stories—a blood-relation of the pen. Each seems, as it were, to voice the people in a manner far more effective, because far more from the inside, than that of Mr Galsworthy when he is dealing with the poor. But Mr Bennett writes with composure as against Mr Wells' enthusiasm. It is very noticeable that Mr Wells' characters never act along the lines of passion, of settled conviction or of reason. Their deeds seem to be dictated by fits of irritability, so that his books have the appearance of being driven along before the winds of brain-storms. This may very well be a characteristic of modern life and we have no particular quarrel with Mr Wells because he renders it. Mr Bennett's books, on the other hand, are more composed in tone and his models have been almost as exclusively French as the writers to whom we have earlier referred. The "Old Wives' Tale" and "Clayhanger" remind us more than anything of "Germinie Lacerteux"—that sombre façade with the sparse lighted windows. It is probable that Mr Bennett has in his work a more composed tone because more than Mr Wells he represents that side of modern life which has left romanticism behind. For modern life has left behind old faiths, old illusions, old chivalries and old heroisms. But at times, and spasmodically, it

chafes after these old and impracticable virtues.   Individuals continue to strive to assert themselves against
the pressure of the body politic : individuals attempt
at times to hold up torches in the general greyness.
And inasmuch as it becomes daily more difficult to
emerge, so the friction of the struggle induces irritability.   It is this tendency in his characters that Mr
Wells so adequately represents for us.   It is, perhaps,
a further stage of our life that Mr Bennett portrays.

It is significant that both these writers, having
evidently a strong desire to give us what is their best
of a non-commercial kind must yet, as it were, pay
their way with writings that each probably regard as
negligible in the extremest sense just as apparently
Mr Galsworthy salves his conscience as a citizen by
whole books or by passages in other books in which
he attempts to uphold the cause of the weak.   The
world, in fact, is too much with us.   It is with us to
such an extent that non-commercial writing is almost
an impossibility to-day.   With the standard and cost
of living increasing daily and with the contempt for
the imaginative writer daily increasing too, it becomes
almost impossible for the novelist to remain the stern
scientist that he should be.   On the one hand, if he
be poor he will seek to snatch some of the joys of life
by means of books which he hopes will tickle the ears
of his inferiors.   Or, on the other hand, he will seek
to palliate the contempt which he feels is bestowed on
his career or to wash away the stigma of effeminacy
which, in a materialistic nation he dimly feels that

being a mere writer confers upon him, by attempting to become a social reformer, a man of action or a censor of the State. The most dismal instance of this last tendency is Mr Rudyard Kipling. In him we have a writer of gifts almost as great as gifts could be. To read merely, let us say, "Stalky & Co." is to be almost overwhelmed by the cleverness in handling incident and in suggesting atmosphere. But at a certain stage of his career Mr Kipling became instinct with the desire to be of importance, with the result that, using his monumental and semi-Biblical language, alternating it with his matchless use of colloquialisms, Mr Kipling set out to attack world problems from the point of view of the journalists' club smoking-room and with the ambitions of a sort of cross between the German Emperor of caricature and a fifth-form public school boy. This is a lamentable record, for in Mr Kipling we seem to have lost for good a poet of the highest vitality, a writer the most emotionally suggestive. For the business of the imaginative writer is to stir up and thus to sweeten and render wholesome the emotions. The mere rendering of human lives is a task so great and so subtle as to call for all the intellectual activity of any given man. He may—indeed he ought to—have within him a reserve of activity for the leading of an active and material life. He may very well use his emotional force in the endeavour to prove a good citizen. For without having lived how can any man write of life ? But his life-work will call for all his intellectual power.

ENGLISH LITERATURE OF TO-DAY

We have treated, of course, only of the writers who are typical of certain movements—of those whom it is possible to classify. For outside the ranks of these two literary schools there remain an infinite number of novelists producing, some of them, work eminently creditable with or without knowledge of what they are actually achieving. And there are, we are well aware, several younger writers whose output, though it has hitherto been limited, has yet maintained a very high level of conscience. But it is obvious that we could do no more than we have done. Our task has been rather to discover whether there did or did not exist in England a school of Literature at all, or whether Literature of to-day was all and altogether a matter of disunited and disordered individual activities without tendencies as without traditions, without standards as without aspirations. And we think we have proved that, in the case of such writers as Mr James, Mr Conrad and Mr George Moore, the great main-stream of European International Literature is cultivating still in England the muses upon a little thin oatmeal. The temperamentally British novel, the loose, amorphous, genial and easy-going thing that was represented by Fielding, by Dickens and by Thackeray, and with more art and less geniality by Anthony Trollope—this thing that is as essentially national as is the English pudding—is a little more difficult to discern. But Mr Wells has his spiritual kinship with Dickens : Mr Kipling is, or perhaps we should say was, a less discursive

THE CRITICAL ATTITUDE

Thackeray. And have we not Mr William de Morgan ? And it should be remembered that a writer is very seldom exactly discernible to his contemporaries. It would be profitless to say that Mr Conrad is a greater writer than Dickens, or Mr Galsworthy a figure bulking more largely than in her day did George Eliot, just as it would be offering hostages to fortune to say that they are smaller. The contemporaries of these writers thought them of comparatively little account compared with others before them whom we have now forgotten. Fitzgerald, for instance, was of opinion that Tennyson never wrote a line of any real value after 1842. And there is no criterion of greatness save the verdict of the future. Indeed every day to attain to any view of contemporary Literature grows more and more difficult. Public taste is no guide, for public taste at one time applauded Shakespeare and at another ignored Keats. And the critics of to-day grow daily more tired, grow daily more negligent, grow daily less inclined to say, as they ought before the opening of each book, that here is a potential Turgenev. They will say upon one day that Mr So-and-so is as great as Thackeray ; upon the morrow they will say the same of Miss ——. But they will, in the one case as in the other, be entirely insincere. So that we have no means of knowing. We have no means of knowing at all. Personally, to sum the matter up, we should say, that, regarded as an art, Literature in England was, at the present moment, on a higher plane than it has attained to for many centuries. In consequence it has lost its appeal to the great people. For Art, which perceives things not visible to the everyday eye, whose truths become apparent only to future generations, can make very little appeal to the everyday mind of its time. The greatest products of Art have sometimes appealed to their own times for one set of reasons and to times unborn for another. Thus Mr Wells might very well appeal to all youth by his ideas or Mr Kipling by his. This is probably what happened in the case of Shakespeare, who apparently regarded his own plays as mere pot-boilers, echoing vulgar catchwords, bristling with popular jokes and topical allusions and beating quite as loudly as Mr Kipling the shrill cymbals of aggressive patriotism. But, the man being dead, these popular attractions became merely so much dry dust, and what was sweet and charming in the personality, what was noble and lofty in the views of life that he held came out from beneath the detritus and showed beautiful as beneath its patina a statue shows. So it may very well be with some writer despised to-day as Shakespeare was despised by the higher literary lights and the smaller hack writers of his age. And, for the matter of that, how can we tell that the manuscript that yesterday editorially we rejected may not contain the first, or for the matter of that, the last writing of a writer greater than the world has ever seen. And the only comment that we can make, the only moral that we can draw is that the writer in days that for him are rather dark, should still, according to his light,

THE CRITICAL ATTITUDE

strive to fulfil what he may regard as the particular canon of his Art. For no one canon of Art is right though one or another may seem to suit itself more nicely to the spirit of an age. But sincerity and a tranquilly fierce enthusiasm of a man set upon expressing to the last word the truth as he sees it—these, though they are not a sure passport to immortality, are the only ones that a writer may find :

> " So, to the measure of the light vouchsafed,
> Shine poet in thy place and be content."

THE PASSING OF
THE GREAT FIGURE

CHAPTER V

THE PASSING OF THE GREAT FIGURE

IN the last chapter we attempted to adumbrate the fact that the great figure as a factor in life has passed almost out of the sphere of things. Conversing largely and frequently with men of varied vocations and pursuits, we have attempted to discover whether, even amongst those who are distinctively specialists, there exist for each of a number of groups any really dominating personalities. And to some extent these may be said to exist. Thus a scientist would give you Sir William Crookes ; a certain group of poets would insist upon the claims of Mr Doughty or of Mr Robert Bridges ; we, ourselves, in speaking of the novel have mentioned Mr Wells and Mr Galsworthy. But at the end of it we imagine that there is only one figure of the present day which has a hold upon the general popular imagination.

We were the other day, at a place of popular entertainment. And it must be remembered that it is in places of popular entertainment, alone, that the pulse of the unthinking can be felt. And that the unthinking—that those who get their views of public questions from a combination of traditional feelings and of the emotions of the moment—that these form the great bulk of our population we can hardly doubt. At public meetings for or against any particular measure or policy the tone of mind shown is of too specialised a character. By some trick of human nature a person inclined to Tariff Reform will attend meetings only which are addressed by Tariff Reform speakers; Socialist orators will attract only Socialists, and as a general rule Suffragettes will listen only to Suffragettes. This is curious, for one might imagine that humanity, anxious to be upon the right side, would also be anxious to hear both. Or one might imagine that humanity, anxious to confute its opponents, would be anxious also to hear the ablest arguments that its opponents possessed. But nothing of the sort. More political causes have been lost by failing to consider what the enemy had up its sleeve in the way of popular appeal than were ever won by fervid and right-minded oratory. The fact is that what humanity desires, passionately and almost before all other things, is a creed. It craves for accepted ideas; it longs for a mind at rest. The moment that questions, social, political, or æsthetic—the moment that questions at all abstract leave the broad ways of black and white, the great bulk of humanity abandons for good the consideration of such questions at all. And nothing is more difficult than, at the present moment, to diagnose the exact condition. All questions have become so exceedingly complicated, there is so little opening for moral fervour that the tendency of the great public

THE PASSING OF THE GREAT FIGURE

is more and more to leave all public matters in the hands of a comparatively few specialists. Practical politics have become so much a matter of sheer figures that the average man, dreading mathematics almost as much as he dreads an open mind, is reduced, nevertheless, to a state of mind so open that he has abandoned thinking—that he has abandoned even feeling about any public matter at all. His vote at a general election will be influenced by some mysterious catchword, by some accidental happening of the moment of by some private scandal or facial characteristic of the upholder of one or other cause.

At the popular entertainment to which we have referred one of the " turns " consisted in the very clever impersonation of a number of prominent personages. When the entertainer announced that he was going to show us Mr Asquith, there began amongst the audience a considerable volume of applause. And this rose to something still more considerable upon the presentation of an excellent counterfeit of the features of the Leader of the Opposition. The announcement that Mr Lloyd George would be shown us was received with applause more considerable than that which had greeted the similar announcement of Mr Balfour. Similarly the applause bestowed upon the impersonation of the Chancellor of the Exchequer was vastly more enthusiastic. A certain number of hisses came from the more expensive seats, but, since it was early in the evening, these were sparsely filled. Mr Burns attracted comparatively little attention.

115

The entertainer then said : " I will now present to your attention a gentleman who is known to all of you." We speculated whilst, with his back to the audience, he was adjusting his wigs and other properties, as to who this gentleman would be. We thought of winning jockeys, of aeroplanists, of foreign Ministers, and of His Majesty the King. The entertainer turned suddenly round and presented us with a cocked-up nose, an eye-glass and an orchid. And from the very places whence there had burst forth an applause of Mr Lloyd George so loud that we had imagined it could not have been surpassed—from those very upper parts of the house there burst forth cries, howls, stamping of feet—a noise of enthusiasm such as reduced the approbation of Mr Lloyd George to a faint platonic sound.

This is a very curious and interesting manifestation, and one which seems to bear strongly on the question of the great figure—for what is the great figure but, in the words of the entertainer, " A gentleman who is known to all of you " ? And, carefully advising with ourselves, we have been unable to think of any other British subject of whom this could remotely be said. Of the Victorian guard of great figures there remain to us only Mr Frederic Harrison and, perhaps, Mr Thomas Hardy. But Mr Thomas Hardy until towards the end of his writing life never made any moral appeal. He was just a writer : he left alone the Riddle of the Universe. And, at bottom, it was by force of crying out, " Be moral and you will have a

good time in one world or another," or it was by force
of providing an alternative for the dogma of seven-
day creation, that the Victorian great figure gained its
prodigious hold upon the hearts of the people.
Tennyson, Browning, Carlyle, Ruskin, Gladstone,
Disraeli, Cobden, Bright, Darwin, John Stuart Mill,
Cardinal Newman, or Mr Frith, whose death occurred
only yesterday—of all these great figures it would be
absurd to say that they did better work in their several
departments than is being done to-day. But they had,
as distinguished from the actual work that they did,
a certain extraneous faculty—the faculty of appeal.
They were able, that is to say, to make a great deal
of noise apart from the actual work that they got
through. Thus Darwin, who has done more to change
the psychology of the Western world than any man
since Jean Jacques Rousseau—Darwin, as far as the
outside world is concerned, was only very secondarily a
scientist. What he stood for was the downfall of priestcraft. Similarly, Mr Gladstone was, for his followers,
not so much a great Chancellor of the Exchequer or the
introducer of certain measures into the House of Commons; he was a man who preached, who stood for virtues
of a certain order. Mill stood for liberty far more than
for political economy. Carlyle for physical force and
public efficiency than for historic sense ; Browning
was the prophet of optimism, Tennyson the singer
of middle-class altruism, Cardinal Newman was a
beloved ascetic rather than an efficient Churchman,
the Prince Consort was Albert the Good. Nowadays

it is the work itself which counts. It counts in the eyes of the worker ; in the eyes of the public, it counts for very little. For the public is always looking out for the great figure.

That is why Mr Chamberlain is the only gentleman whom every one knows—for Mr Chamberlain does stand for an enormous principle. He pays comparatively little attention to detail ; he never did pay much attention to detail. The note which he sounded when he was a Radical was one of emotional common sense. The note which he sounds to-day is that of emotional patriotism. But the emotion which he used then as now was not an emotion of altruism. It was one of a rather black, a rather bitter aggressiveness. For it should have been visible to the Darwinians and to the Victorians when, fairly efficiently, they slew priestcraft and revealed religion, they scotched also several of the things for which priestcraft and revealed religion seemed to stand. Thus, if, as has been said, Protestantism is dead, so also is altruism. We do not wish to assert finally that either of these facts is the case. But we are fairly certain that for the time being and until others arise the great Victorian figures were the last of the priests.

Darwinism, however, shook so severely all the traditional standards, whether of religion, of ethics or of morals till that time existing, that although the great figures of Darwin's age functioned along the lines of those traditions their priestly glamour vanished with the passing of themselves and their contemporaries.

THE PASSING OF THE GREAT FIGURE

The conditions of everyday life and thought have changed so entirely that we very much doubt whether a Ruskin or a Gladstone would to-day find any kind of widespread dominion. Divergent views find to-day such an easy expression that the mind at all inquiring is perpetually driven now in one direction, now in another. In the Victorian Era an official altruism reigned as the unquestioned standard whether of the religious or of the agnostic—a sentimental altruism embracing all humanity, all races, all types. To-day, although in the one column of a newspaper, as it were, we may read the altruist dogma that the province of good government is to work for the greatest good of the greatest number, in another column or half-way down the same column under another heading we shall see advocated the employment of the lethal chamber for the feeble-minded. And it will not be so very long before advocates will be found—advocates serious and public—for the extinction, painless or otherwise, of the physically weak, of the unemployed, or even of the merely unfortunate. We have, of course, no desire to advocate the claims of the one or the other school of thought. But whether the true end of government be the raising up of the weak or the improvement of opportunity for the strong, we must resign ourselves to the fact that both sides will find expression and almost equal opportunities for expression. And in between the two extremes will be found innumerable shades of opinion, each shade finding its expression and contributing to the obscuring of the issues. And this produces in the public mind a weariness, a confusion that leads in the end to something amounting almost to indifference. Thus, supposing that Mr Gladstone should nowadays call attention to misrule in Macedonia, he might very well find a tendency upon part of the public to say that the Macedonians are one of the weak races of the world, and that the sooner and the more efficiently they are stamped out the better it will be for a world which is already growing over-populated. Or—and this is still more likely—he might find that the public mind was utterly unable to make the effort to interest itself at all in the matter of Macedonia. Of course, in the question of oppressed peoples, as in all other questions, certain technical factors operate to produce special results. Thus, supposing for Mr Gladstone championing the cause of Macedonia we substitute the figure of Mr Ruskin championing the cause of certain neglected artists, Mr Ruskin would be met with an indifference certainly more profound than that accorded to the champion of oppressed peoples. For, on the one hand, to the Victorians the figures of Chatterton starving in a garret and of Keats pining and dying beneath the lash of the *Quarterly* reviewer —to the Victorian these figures disappearing so miserably, to be so gloriously revived by a posterity that was the Victorians themselves—these figures had about them something great, romantic, and glorious. Art, too, had about itself still a sort of super-glamour due to its comparative rareness. But nowadays we cannot discover any lately deceased Chattertons or Keatses. If we did discover them we should regard their discoverers with suspicion. And the mind is being so perpetually diverted by new topics that we could not for very long keep before us either the figure of Keats or Chatterton, either of Macedonia or of any of the oppressed peoples. It is not so much that we are languid as that the public brain cannot by any possibility, under the perpetual claims, under the perpetual assaults upon its attention, remain for very long steadfast to any particular subject. There is a perpetual conflict in the public mind between personal problems and public causes. Thus, two years ago the execution of Señor Ferrer raised an enormous storm throughout Europe. Yet within how very few days was its place taken by another trial—the breaking upon a wheel of Madame Steinheil ? Here certain broad emotions of a publicly altruist kind are wiped out by others of a more or less intimate nature. Señor Ferrer represented . liberty, democracy, the rights of free speech, and a whole group of kindred human aspirations. Madame Steinheil was a woman who, having conceded that her antecedents were not of the most savoury, battled manfully to save her neck from the guillotine and her fame from the most horrible aspersions in the midst of a mystery that she alone could really unravel. And we can imagine a very proper man and a very good citizen saying : " I should be more than human if the case of Señor Ferrer occupied the whole of my attention : I should be less than human if I devoted no thought at all to Madame Steinheil."

For, after all, the province of the proper man is to say : " *Nihil humanum a me alienum puto.*" And that being so, how is he to-day to discriminate ? He will have to decide on one and the same morning what he thinks as to the attitude of the House of Lords towards the Budget, and as to the successful beating of the height record by the latest aviator ; he will have to consider the state of the Navy and as to whether British-owned masterpieces should be prevented from leaving the country, and, if so, how the prevention is to be brought about. He will have, in addition, other private interests. He may have brought before his mind the latest play at the Haymarket, the quarrels between the professionals and the Football Association, the form of probable starters for the Grand National, the rival claims of two explorers, or the latest publication by a resident of Harley Street of a new diet. There will also be an infinite number of still more trifling matters, each claiming its share of his attention.

And though none of these things is in itself of necessity below the attention of an efficient member of society—though, indeed, the most hard-thinking of us may, and possibly should, have his small relaxations, his hobbies, and the childishnesses with which he will keep his soul sweet, the tendency of the public Press is to force the relatively unimportant things, in a perpetually flickering cloud of small claims upon the attention, into the foreground. We are not, of course, intent upon considering which of these human matters is unimportant. It would be pharisaic to say that a large portion of humanity is reprehensible because it takes an interest in the fate or in the struggle of Madame Steinheil. But there can be no doubt that the thought and the capacity for thinking thoughts are of very great importance to humanity. Thus, though the disappearance of the great figure is not in itself a thing to be wholly lamented, yet since this disappearance is, as much as anything, a symptom of a disease of thoughtlessness it is almost wholly to be lamented. For, for a man who is at all interested in the manifestations of his day, any connected thought is almost a matter of impossibility. At the same time, for a thinker to withdraw himself from the life of his day is almost a fatal matter. It is a fatal matter not so much because he will become a specialist as because he will lack the corrective influence of irreverential contact with his kind. If he is a person of distinction he will gather round him a small body of sycophants, who, by applauding his every word, will exaggerate all those of his tendencies that are capable of exaggeration. If, on the other hand, he find neither followers nor admirers he will become the most disastrous of things, a crabbed, solitary introspective.

And the case is even worse with his public. For the public of any man must necessarily be less of the thinker in his special department than he himself will be. And thought, that exercise of the brain, has always been and always must be a painful matter to the average citizen of these islands. The Englishman, as a rule, is like a schoolboy ; if his master is invested with sufficient authority or has a sufficient moral prestige to claim his attention, the ordinary Englishman will, laboriously and with some disinclination, follow the train of thought that is prescribed for him. And the great figure of the Victorian Age was very much in the position of a school-master endowed with great moral prestige. Thus, almost every house of the city merchant or of the Lancashire employer of labour during the latter years of last century would be found to contain a copy of the later works of Browning or of Ruskin. And these volumes—"Asolando" or "Sesame and Lilies"—would be laboriously perused by a head of the house, whose attitude at such times would very much resemble that of a fourth-form schoolboy painfully reading through the "Bacchae" of Euripides. This attitude of the commercial man of the nineteenth century was the last dying survival of the mediæval superstition that something occult attached to Learning, that something profoundly and materialistically valuable attached itself to Thought. Nowadays that feeling is altogether dead. It seemed to die—as we have elsewhere said—with the war in South Africa. And for this there was very good reason. For it was the struggle with the Boers that made the fortune of the more frivolous Press. And it was in those days that the Englishman found a necessity for existence in the snatching of news, turning swiftly from one short sensational paragraph to another, and filling his mind with the sharp facets of facts hardly at all related the one with the other. And having come through that engrossing and protracted trouble he had acquired the habit so strongly that he has never abandoned it. It should be remembered that the South African War was the first vital struggle that this nation has been engaged in since the telegraphic Press was really organised. Before that time, though this tendency was gradually dying, the public was accustomed to accept with equanimity news that was a day or two old—to accept it with equanimity and to ponder over it for some small length of time. But nowadays, even in remote country districts, the Englishman is overwhelmed every morning with a white spray of facts—facts more or less new, more or less important, more or less veracious. And the commercial man who in the old days read his Browning or his Ruskin as a duty now equally as a duty plays his round of golf to increase his physical well-being, since this perusal of facts will have stilled that position of his mind that craves for the printed page. Moreover, it should be remembered, the chief purpose of Thought as of the Arts is the promotion of expression between man and man. And whereas in former days conversation concerned itself, for lack of other topics, more frequently than not with the latest book or the latest idea, to-day the world appears to be so full of a number of things material, technical, or of gossip that there is no necessity, in whatever rank of life, for conversation to flag for one minute. This is, of course, a somewhat exaggerated statement of facts. It is probable—though this is somewhat difficult to ascertain, and may be merely a matter of opinion—that, as far as numbers are concerned, in certain strata of Society or in certain individuals scattered up and down amongst all ranks there might be, if they could be collected, a number of persons anxious to be presented with generalised and ordered thought—a number as great as existed in the nineties of the last century. What has been lost from the comfortable classes has probably been gained or more than gained by the spread of education amongst the comparatively penurious. Indeed amongst this latter class we have found from experience that there is probably a greater desire for serious literature than amongst the former. But the fact remains that the production of thought is a costly process. The thinker must be educated in a very expensive manner, and the machinery of putting his thoughts before the public is also expensive in the extreme. This calls into play, even before the thinker will have made a bare subsistence—this calls into play the capitalist. And the object of the capitalist is, reasonably enough, not so much the cultivation of a not very small, not very wealthy circle, but the obtaining of an infinite number of small profits and of quick returns. An immense reading public has come into existence, and the desire of those who cater for it is not to promote thought, but to keep it entertained. In this way it becomes increasingly difficult even so much as to attract in any way the attention of the few who think, drowned as they are amidst the immense multitude of those who have learned no more than to desire to be entertained.

There is, moreover, a general suspicion of all generalised thought abroad in the land to-day. Rightly or wrongly, the general thinker—the man whose speculations cover wide fields—is regarded with suspicion by the world. Versatility is taken to be an evidence of shallowness, and the mind which occupies itself with more than one subject is suspected of a want of application. From one point of view this is a good thing. It means to say that if the public has not yet learned to detect the charlatan it has at least progressed sufficiently far to suspect facile workmanship. Thus two contending forces are everywhere at work. Upon the one hand we are creating specialists everywhere ; we will listen to none but specialists. Upon the other we are making it commercially almost impossible for the specialist to exist at all. We will listen to no one else : we will hardly listen to him. And this tendency is as visible in material things as in the world of thought. Just as the large public gets its ideas from syndicated presses, so it gets its bodily nourishment from what are called " canned goods " and proprietary articles. A medical officer of health of one of the poorer districts of London has informed us that most of those amongst whom he worked had acquired, if not an actual distaste for cooked meat, at least an actual preference for potted articles that were either eaten cold or could easily be heated up. In the same district, baker's shops are comparatively rare, mothers preferring to give their children cheap sweet cakes which had been manufactured by great companies. They avoid thus both the trouble of spreading bread with butter and the expense of the butter itself, butter being one of the most costly articles of diet in general use. Thus, the cook, who is the specialist of every household, is being more and more dispensed with throughout the land, just as the jam, cordial, and preserve-maker has disappeared from the household of the comfortable. And throughout country towns the specialist tradesman, who used to flourish in considerable numbers, is starved out if he is unfortunate, or converts his business into a limited company, amalgamating it with others, reducing his prices, as a rule deteriorating the quality of the commodity that he produces, or, at the best, depriving his commodity of his personal touch.

There are those who deplore this tendency : there are those who see in it a great hope for the future. On the one hand it becomes increasingly difficult for the consumer to know where to go to procure those things which impart all the finer flavour to life ; for the producer, whether of Thought or of liqueurs, it becomes increasingly difficult to gain a subsistence by giving to his ware the attraction of the finer flavour. He must either reconcile himself to starvation or make the attempt to appeal to a market relatively uneducated. The old order, in fact, is changing ; the new has hardly visibly arrived. On the other hand, the Modernists say that this is only democracy getting ready to do its work. The great popular taste, they say, is only whetting itself with these trifles and sweetmeats. It is getting ready to think higher thoughts, to read and to produce nobler books, to clamour for finer food, to lead more beautiful lives. We are not, these enthusiasts claim, so much at the end of an old era as at the beginning of one when all that is beautiful in old things will be multiplied a thousandfold and spread abroad through the land. It is true that the cheap reprint has almost stopped the production of the better class of original new work. On the other hand, the cheap reprint is spreading in its millions throughout the country examples of a very much better class of work than was prevalent in any cheap form in the day when the penny dreadful reigned alone. Nay, more : it is creating a million-fold of new readers, it is creating readers that never before existed. And these readers, having begun with, having become cloyed by works of an amiable mediocrity, will go on to demand in a thousand places the works inspired by the older and finer spirit. The old great figure is dead, the present finer specialist is starving to death. In years a long way ahead there may rise up a great many of finer specialists, each one of whom will be a Great Figure. This is all the hope there is for Thought and for the Arts.

THE
TWO SHILLING NOVEL

CHAPTER VI

THE TWO SHILLING NOVEL

THE world of letters in England is, perhaps, always in a critical condition, but certain crises of the economic aspect of writing do undoubtedly stand out. And it is to the effect of the financial side of Literature upon the quality of writing that we wish, for the moment, to devote our attention. Certain questions may be asked : Is the writer at his best when shivering in a garret, having sent his breeches to the pawnshop, by the light of a guttering candle stuck in a bottle, upon sugar-paper he indites deathless words ? Or is he at his best when, a Civil Service employé at the Board of Trade or at the Inland Revenue Office, he produces minor verse, Art criticism or annotations of writers who have preceded him by a couple of centuries ? Or again, is he at his best when, with a comfortable fortune at his disposal, with a fine library at his command, say, from Lausanne, he directs his literary operations with a peer as his agent ? Alas ! in England we are familiarised with the dictum that Literature is a good stick but a bad crutch, just as in France, they have the figure of the goat of M. Seguin " qui se battegué touta la nieue émé lo loup, et piei lo matin lo loup l'a manzé." And inasmuch as the great bulk of humanity is not in the fortunate possession of sufficient unearned increment to maintain itself, and to rejoice the heart of the Chancellor of the Exchequer, so the great bulk of humanity being desirous of expressing itself by means of letters, the large majority of writers are those who walk with the aid of this crutch, who fight all night against the wolf. And then in the morning the wolf eats them.

The wolf eats them, the wolf has always eaten them, and, voraciously, the wolf will continue to swallow them down. That, of course, is a matter which does not interest the public : perhaps it should not interest the public. But officially the public is interested in the quality of the literature that reaches it. Cabinet Ministers tell us that this is so at dinners of the Royal Literary Fund, at Academy banquets and in other places where they speak. But complacently the public continues to steal the bread from the mouths of the heirs of men of letters, and to read the half-penny papers. In these islands literature has never come into its own ; perhaps never will, perhaps never can. Probably it never can, since, our public being strictly utilitarian, it cannot be proved that reading imaginative literature ever led to the invention of the steamboat, the gaining of a new colony for the British Crown, the improvement of the morals of Society, or the extension of the Franchise. In short, in the minds of engineers, empire-builders and moral or social reformers in this country, imaginative literature occupies no place at all. In France a man will inscribe himself in an hotel register as *homme de lettres* and be received by the host with effusion. In England, on the other hand, your political agent, of whichever party, calls upon the man of letters as upon other qualified householders or lodgers. But hearing that his prospective supporter is an author he will say with a deprecating, polite smile : " Oh, please put yourself down gentleman." This more favourably impresses the revising barrister.

These, however, are only the generally prevailing conditions. At the present moment, there is a crisis in the book trade. The price of the novel is to be reduced. The novel is to be sold by the pound. One publisher, with a candour which removes his action from the category of sheer cynicism, has adopted the design of a pair of scales for his device and for his motto he has taken the words : " Just weight is a delight." So that we presume, if he should print so many hundred pages of " printer's pie " upon lead-glazed paper he would have a masterpiece worth selling at ten shillings per volume. There is no escape from this deduction ; and, indeed, the first book published by Mr Heinemann under this new dispensation, Mr Hall Caine's " The White Prophet " was a sufficient proof that if Mr Heinemann has his way quantity not quality shall be the distinguishing factor of the book of the future.

We have the less hesitation in mentioning Mr Heinemann by name as it was he who, at a public dinner, first promulgated this dictum. He said, as far as we can remember, that the book of high but condensed quality was nowadays so exceedingly rare that for commercial purposes it might be altogether neglected. And this is a very serious pronouncement to the consideration of which we will return later. But it is, at any rate, a reversal of the former policies of Mr Heinemann and of all the reputable publishers in London. With this earlier policy we have never had any quarrel. Indeed, when advising those about to start publishing we have always held this policy up as the only possible, as the only commendable course to be pursued. It has consisted in publishing, when available, enormously popular but absolutely worthless writers and devoting a certain portion of the profits made by these publications to the production of work that has literary merits and very small commercial attractiveness. It is lamentable that worthless work should be popular, but for that not the publisher but the public—the persons in high places, the preachers, the social reformers and all the rest of those who have the power to influence the public—are responsible.

And even if this were not the case—if, that is to say, the publisher of repute did not adopt as a settled and public-spirited policy the subsidising of good work by work of the most worthless—the inevitable pressure of circumstances would squeeze out of existence any publisher who published good work at all, supposing him not by luck to hit upon a popular author. The following figures may go to substantiate this view. A certain publisher who kindly put his books at our disposal published in a late season thirteen novels. These thirteen had a collected sale of 54,000 copies, or an average of 4000 a piece, but one of those books sold a little over 40,000 copies, and another 6000, leaving to the remaining eleven novels a sale of about 8000 copies. On these figures his accounts showed a considerable profit though actually his losses upon the eleven novels amounted to about £600, without taking into account his expenses for offices, staff, etc. The book which sold 40,000 copies was one of comparatively little literary value. Indeed it had no literary value at all. But it was a quite earnest work calling in a sensational manner the attention of the public to a social evil. The work which sold 6000 copies was of a higher literary value; it had, indeed, even an appreciable interest from the point of view of craftsmanship, of handling, of what is called " technique." But the main appeal of this book, as of the other, was sociological. It was concerned with the difference between classes, with the hard lot of the poor : it was, in short, an " improving " book. One of the other books was a work of extreme merit, but since it consisted of short stories its sale was the lowest, but two of the books in the publisher's list. This the publisher had anticipated, but he had desired to have the author's name in his advertisements in order that his own name might not stink too redolently in the nostrils of the literary world.

THE CRITICAL ATTITUDE

The other works were, in the majority, the ordinary novel of commerce, but the season being a bad one in the book trade, they practically all of them failed in appeal. Three, however, were by unknown writers, the publisher's adviser having recommended their publication, not because there was any probabil:ty of their proving remunerative, but because they showed promise, or because it would be a pleasure and a credit to publish them.

This, upon the whole, is a reputable record. It was, moreover, a profitable one. For whereas the profit upon a novel selling from 800 to 1200 copies is relatively small, it becomes relatively enormous in the case of one selling 40,000 copies, since in the latter case the cost of composition is an infinitesimal percentage and there remain, to all intents and purposes, only those of machining, of paper and of binding. For, when once a book is really started upon a " boom," advertising may be stopped altogether. Thus it was infinitely more profitable to have the two sales at 40,000 and 6000 and the eleven small sales than to have had the sales distributed over thirteen books at the rate of 4000 a piece.

What then will be the effect of reducing the published price of a novel to two shillings—or of selling novels by weight ? In the first place, it must lead to the absolute extinction of the finest class of work, since the finest class of work is that in which every superfluous word is meticulously excised, in which every episode is of value to the story. We are familiar enough already with the old-fashioned tyranny of the bookseller who demanded from the publisher that every novel should be of the length of 75,000 words at least. This demand has led to the virtual extinction of what is almost the most beautiful length for any history of an episode—as distinguished from the history of an "affair" involving the life-stories of many persons — that of from 30,000 to 40,000 words. For this type of story there is practically no place for publication at all in England now. It is too short to be published in volume form : bound up with other stories it becomes catalogued with and unsaleable as "Short Stories" : the magazines will not print it since it is too short to be a serial, and too long to go in one or two instalments. In consequence, and simply owing to commercial pressure, this particular form is practically extinct. Yet it is one which, on the face of it, should be particularly suited to the English genius. For the Englishman appears to be almost incapable of producing the real short story—the *conte*. He has not the technical skill necessary for getting the best out of his subject, and his especial genius being what is called "getting an atmosphere," he is utterly incapable of getting an atmosphere in a few words. He must have his initial page or two for the description of Dartmoor, Cork Castle, the Mile End Road, a drawing-room in Mayfair or the environs of Trincomalee. And having in this leisurely way made himself feel at home, he is then fit to deal in an equally leisurely manner with the human affairs of his episode. Of course it would be unreasonably arbitrary to say that all episodes must be treated of, at, or under the length of 40,000 words, or that all "affairs" must have devoted to them two hundred or more, thousand words. But, as a rough generalisation, we may say that there is no settled form that is really satisfactory between the length of, say Flaubert's "Cœur Simple" and that of his "Education Sentimentale." The latter work Mr Heinemann would welcome with open arms, the former he would condemn.

And if the present state of things is unsatisfactory for the writer of a fine conscience and a talent for compression, the revolution which Mr Heinemann initiated and which almost every other publisher in London is, in secret, prepared to take part in—this revolution will prove infinitely worse. What these publishers are really doing is to attempt to compete with the sevenpenny reprint, an attempt foolish in itself the moment one considers that the public is quite well aware that it can procure any new book for the price of about one halfpenny from its circulating library. The public, in fact, is an almost negligible quantity as far as works of the imagination are concerned. Figures fluctuate a little, but we believe it is fairly safe to say that of the works of fiction and *belles-lettres* published every year only twenty per cent. are purchased by the booksellers, the rest going to the circulating libraries. Now these figures should give a publisher furiously to think, for they represent all of the book-buying class who must, either for pleasure or for ⁓ofit, possess works of the imagination. The libraries, obviously, must have the books, or they would lose their customers ; and so rare is it for an Englishman to purchase a book that we must imagine that the remaining twenty per cent. must be impelled to this expenditure by some irresistible force. And the publisher, in the face of this helpless body, instead of putting up his prices, puts them down. It seems like a policy of madness. It is a policy that certainly will profit nobody but the libraries. For one factor which the publishers always forget is that of time. If a man feels himself rich, healthy and prosperous he will eat more beef, drink more wine, purchase more clothes, and order new motor-cars, but neither health nor wealth can give a man more time for reading. And the amount of time the public can, or will give to reading is now entirely taken up. The consequence is that Mr Heinemann's *confrères* will be giving to a market, already strictly circumscribed, an article of greater quantity, of almost inevitably lower quality and certainly smaller price. The writer without a conscience will spin his works out to enormous length : the normally long-winded author will obtain a smaller honorarium : the author who seeks for artistic restraint and conciseness will find no form of publication at all. For the immediate result of a reduction in prices must be very much to limit the output of books. The publisher, for the mere reasons of the size of his staff, the cost of distribution and the comparative smallness of his profit, must tend more and more to put his eggs into one basket, and that one basket must be that ingeniously woven by a "safe" author. And the "safe" author, whatever he be, can never, in England, be the author of literary merit. That, the quality being equal, a book three times as long stands three times as much chance of success as a shorter book we are inclined to believe—simply because the book taking longer to read, the libraries, to satisfy their customers with some approach to despatch, must obviously purchase a larger number of copies and, indeed, the most egregiously popular of our present-day novelists do, as a rule, put forth yearly volumes of an intolerable length. And the poor publisher, confronted with these great bulks of matter, his offices filled with copies awaiting distribution, will find his profits reduced to almost nothing — for it is impossible to imagine that three times as many people will be found to spend in reading the works of Mr Hall Caine, Miss Marie Corelli and the other writers of the stamp, three times as much time as is at present spent over these normally enormous productions. And having no space for the unsold copies of writers of definite merit, but of only problematic commercial value, the poor publisher will be forced to let his good name go by the board ; no longer will Mr Henry James save the face of the gentleman who publishes Miss Corelli, no longer will Mr Doughty's name be weighed in the balance against Mrs Elinor Glynn,

THE TWO SHILLING NOVEL

no longer will the white and innocent candour of publishing Mr Joseph Conrad cover the purple blush of shame that will come at the thought of having poured innumerable copies of Mr Caine's work upon the world.

THE WOMAN OF THE
NOVELISTS

CHAPTER VII

THE WOMAN OF THE NOVELISTS

An open Letter, To . . . . . .

M Y DEAR MESDAMES, X, Y, AND Z.
We should like you to observe that
we are writing to you not on the women, but
on the Woman of the novelists. The distinction is
very deep, very serious. If we were writing on female
characters—on the women of the novelists—we should
expect to provide a series of notes on the female
characters of our predecessors or our rivals. We
should say that Amelia (Fielding's Amelia) was too
yielding, and we should look up Amelia and read
passages going to prove our contention. Or we should
say we envied Tom Jones—and again give our reasons
for that envy. We should say that Amelia Osborne
(Thackeray's Amelia) was a bore. And we should
bore you with passages about Amelia. We should
flash upon you Clarissa and Pamela ; Portia and the
patient Grisel ; Di Vernon and Lady Humphrey's
Daughter (perhaps that is not the right title) ; Rose
(from "Evan Harrington")—we adore Rose and very
nearly believe in her—and Mr Haggard's "She." We

THE CRITICAL ATTITUDE

should in fact try to present you with a series of " Plutarch's Lives " in tabloid form, contrasting Amelia Osborne with Fielding's Amelia ; Rose Harrington with Lady Rose's Daughter (we have got the title right this time) or Portia with the heroine of " What Maisie Knew." It would be fun and if would be quite easy : we should just have to write out a string of quotations, and there would be an end of it.

But the " Woman of the Novelists " is quite other guess work. It is analysis that is called for—analysis that is hard to write and harder to read. To put it as clearly as we can, all the women of the novelists that you have read make up for you the Woman of the Novelists. She is, in fact, the creature that you average out as woman.

For you who are women, this creature is not of vast importance as an object lesson. For us men she is of the utmost. We fancy that, for most of us she is the only woman that we really know. This may seem to some of you an extravagant statement. Let us examine it a little more closely.

Has it occurred to you to consider how few people you really know ?—How few people, that is to say, there are whose biographies, whose hearts, whose hopes, whose desires and whose fears you have really known and sounded ! As you are women and a good many of you are probably domestic women, this will not appear to you as clear as it will to most men. Yet it will be clear enough. Let us put a case—the case we know best—our own, in fact.

THE WOMAN OF THE NOVELISTS

We have a way of putting ourselves to sleep at night by indulging in rather abstruse mental calculations. Lately we figured out for ourselves how many people we know, however slightly. The limits we set were that we should know their names, be able to sit next them at table. We could reckon up rather over a thousand—to be exact, one thousand and forty.

But of all of these how many do we really *know* ? The figure that we have arrived at may seem a little preposterous, but we have considered them rather carefully. We know intimately the circumstances and the aspirations of eight men and two women and we are bound to say that both women say we do not understand them. Still for the purposes of our argument we will say that we do.

In the present-day conditions of life, as we have said, men are more prone to these acquaintanceships that are not knowledge. They go to business and negotiate with great numbers of simulacra in the shape of men. Some have eyes, beards, voices, humours and tempers ; some are merely neckties, waistcoats or penholders. But as to how these simulacra live, what they really desire—apart from their functional desires to outwit us in the immediate business in hand—as to what they are as members of society, we have, as a rule, no knowledge at all.

We meet at our club every day from twenty to thirty men of whose circumstances we have not the least idea. One of them is, for instance, quite good company, distinguished and eminently conversational.

THE CRITICAL ATTITUDE

We know what his public function is : we know his politics : we know his vices. But as for knowing *him* : why, we have never even looked him up in " Who's Who " to see if he is married !

And, if we are so walled off from men, how much more are we walled off from women ? I should say that, out of that odd thousand acquaintances, about six hundred are women. Yet the conventions of modern life prevent us from really knowing more than two—and those two, we are told, we do not understand.

We daresay we don't. But who is to blame ? Why, the Woman of the Novelists.

We trust that, by now, you know what we are driving at.

For the conditions of modern life are such that for experience of our fellow men we have to go almost entirely to books. And the books that we go to for this knowledge are those of the imaginative writers.

(Thus among novelists—or the greatest of English novelists — we should include Shakespeare. We should also include Chaucer and perhaps the English dramatists up to Sheridan — the dramatists like Congreve, that is, who are read and not performed. We have reasons for making these inclusions that we will not dwell upon.)

We may take ourself to be the average man : the man in the street. And you will find that the man in the street—or rather the men on your hearthstones —your husbands and brothers—are in much the same case as ourself. You will find that they know up to a score or so of men. You will—if you are the average wife—take care that they don't know more than a couple of women, one of them being yourself. And you will all agree with us when we say that your husbands and your brothers do not understand you. They think they do ; but they do not. Poor simple, gross creatures, for them two and two will be four. For you—I wonder how much two and two are ?

Yet your man of the hearthstone will talk about woman. He will talk about her with a simple dogmatism, with a childish ·arrogance. He will tread on all your corns. He will say that women are incapable of humour. (Of course, in his mind he will exclude you and his sister and mother—but he will never make you believe that.) He will say that women are changeable. (He will probably include you in that.) He will say that every woman is at heart a rake. (We do not know where you come in there.) He will say that a certain lane is called Dumb Woman's Lane because it is so steep that no woman's feet ever carried her up it. Well, you know all about what he will say as well as we do.

But you observe : he is talking about Woman ; he talks with the confidence of an intimate. But what woman is it that he talks of ? Why is it that you are not torn with pangs of jealousy when he thus speaks ? Who is this creature ; incapable of humour, steadfastness, virtue or reticence ? You are not alarmed : you do not suddenly say to yourself : " Are these the women he spends his time with when he pretends to

be at his office, his club, his golf-links or his tailor's ? "
You are quite tranquil on that account; you hate
him for his conceit, but you know you have him safe.
This is no woman of prey that he is analysing. Women
of prey are more attractive: they bewilder, they
ensnare, they do not leave room for dogmatism. No,
This is the Woman of the Novelist!

We do not mean to say that there have never been
men whose views of women were founded upon actual
experience, who took lines of their own and adhered
to them. There have even been imaginative writers
who have done this : there have been, that is to say,
misogynists, as there have been women worshippers,
and there have been a few men to whom the
eternal feminine presents eternal problems for
curiosity.

We do not recall, at this moment, any great
novelist who has actually been a misogynist: it
would indeed be a little difficult to write a novel
from a misogynistic point of view—though there are
several novelists who come as nearly as is possible
to a pitch of altogether ignoring the Fair Sex.

The Fair Sex! Do not these two words bring
to mind the greatest of all misogynists—Arthur
Schopenhauer ? For, says he, that we should call
the narrow-chested, broad hipped, short-legged,
small waisted, low-browed, light-brained tribe, the
Fair Sex, is that not a proof of the Christo-
Germanic stupidity from which all we Teutons
suffer ?

THE WOMAN OF THE NOVELISTS

We wonder how many of you have read Schopenhauer's " Über die Weiber " ?   If you have not you should certainly do so.   It is an indictment of what —owing to various causes—women may sink to.   It is, of course, exaggerated ; but it is savagely witty in the extreme.   (And, if it enrage you, go on to read the other monograph in " Parerga and Paralipomena " in which Schopenhauer attacks carters who crack whips.   " Über Lärm und Geräusch " it is called. There you will see that what Schopenhauer attacks —along with one type of woman—is the middling sorts of men.)

The one type of woman that he attacks—the garrulous, light-headed, feather-brained type that he says includes all woman-kind—this one type was drawn from the one woman from whom Schopenhauer really suffered.   Schopenhauer was—his pasquinades apart—a mystic and dogged thinker, and the thinker is apt to consider that his existence is the all important thing in this world—and that the disturber of his existence is the greatest of criminals.

The one woman from whom he suffered was his mother.   All other women he stalled off ; his mother he could not.   And Johanna Schopenhauer was what you might call a terror.

To begin with, for a considerable portion of Schopenhauer's life, she held the purse strings.   She was an indomitable, garrulous creature.   (Need we say that she was one of the most successful women novelists of her day ?) She had the power to approach Schopenhauer at all times : to talk to him incessantly : to reproach this needy and lofty thinker with his want of success as a writer : to recommend him to follow her example and become a successful novelist.

So that, actually, it was his mother's type that he was attacking when he thought—or pretended to think—that he was attacking all womenkind. And that, upon the whole, is what has happened to most of the few writers who have systematically attacked women. We do not think, as we have said, that there are many of these, but some writers have had rather narrow escapes. There was, for instance, Gustave Flaubert.

Flaubert was several times pressed to marry, but he always refused and he gave his reason that : "Elle pourrait entrer dans mon cabinet "—" She might come into my study." From this you will observe that he found just such another woman as was Johanna Schopenhauer. And indeed it *was* just such another —the lady he called La Muse—that he found. The Muse was the only woman with whom he came really into contact—and she was a popular novelist, a writer of feuilletons and of fashion pages, an incessant chatterer. She was no doubt a sufficiently attractive woman to tempt Flaubert towards a close union. But his own wisdom and the fact that she plagued him incessantly to read her manuscripts let him save himself with a whole skin. He was not minded to give her the right—or at any rate the power—to come into his study.

If he had done so—who knows?—under the incessant stimulus of her presence he might have joined the small band of writers who have been women haters.

As it is he was—not so much a misanthropist—a hater of his kind as a lover of what is shipshape He had in fact The Critical Attitude. And seeing how badly—how stupidly—the affairs of this world are governed — this loving the Shipshape rendered him perpetually on the look-out for the imbecilities of poor humanity.

If he was hard upon women, he was harder, without doubt, upon men. Madame Bovary is idle, silly, hyper-romantic, unprincipled, mendacious—but she is upon the whole more true to her poor little lights than most of the male characters of the book—than Homais the quack, than her two lovers—and she is less imbecile than her husband. And indeed, the most attractive and upon the whole the wisest in the conduct of life and in human contacts—the most attractive and wisest character that Flaubert ever drew is Madame Arnoux in "L'Education Sentimentale." She is nearly a perfect being, recognising her limitations and fulfilling her functions. I do not think that Flaubert drew more than one other such—the inimitable Félicité, the patient household drudge, in the "Cœur Simple." Bouvard and Pécuchet are lovable buffoons or optimists, brave and impracticable adventurers into the realms of all knowledge: these two dear men are one or the other as you look at them. Flaubert drew them lovingly but we are not certain that he loved them; it is impossible to doubt that he loved Madame Arnoux, the lady, and Félicité of the Simple Soul. He drew each of them as being efficient—and since he drew two efficient women, and no efficient man at all—we may consider him to have given us the moral that, in an imbecile world, as he saw it, woman had a better chance than man.

We are not quite certain whether we regard Flaubert or Turgenev as having been the greatest novelist the world ever produced. If we introduce a third name—that of Shakespeare—we grow a little more certain. For we should hesitate to say that Flaubert was greater than Shakespeare—in fact we are sure we should not say it—but we are pretty certain that Turgenev was.

His personality was more attractive than Flaubert's —and his characters are more human than Shakespeare's were. So we should give the palm of the supreme writer to Turgenev — and so, we fancy, would every woman if she were wise. For Turgenev was a great lover—a great champion—of women. He was a great lover—a great champion, too, we may say—of humanity. Where Flaubert saw only that humanity was imbecile, Turgenev, kindlier and more sympathetic, saw generally that men were gullible and ineffectual angels. And it is significant that all the active characters—all the persons of action—in Turgenev's novels are women, There is just one man of action—of mental and political action—in all Turgenev's works—and that man, Solomin, the workman agitator, is the one great failure of all Turgenev's projections. He is wooden and unconvincing, an abstractly invented and conventional figure.

And this preponderance of the Fair Sex in Turgenev's action does not come about because Turgenev was a champion of women : it arises simply because of the facts of Russian life as Turgenev saw them. (And let us offer you as an argument, when you are most confounded with the dogma that women never *did* anything political, the cases of Russia and Poland. For, when the history of the Russian Revolution comes to be written it will be seen that an enormous proportion of the practical organising work of the revolution was done by women, the comparatively ineffectual theorising has been in the main the work of men. As for Poland—the Polish national spirit has been kept alive almost solely by the women.)

So with Turgenev : if you take such a novel as " The House of Gentlefolk " you will find that it is Lisa who is the active character, taking a certain course which she considers as the course of duty and persevering in it. Her lover, Lavretsky, on the other hand, is an ineffectual being, resigned if you will, but resigned to the action of destiny. And, roughly speaking, this is the case with all Turgenev's

THE CRITICAL ATTITUDE

characters. It is Bazaroff the Nihilist who is in the hands of the woman he loves: it is only in the physical activities of the peasants that the man takes the upper hand.

But Turgenev, if he was a great lover of women, did not idealise them. We love Lisa with a great affection: she might be our patient but inflexible sister: we love her and believe in her because she is the creation of a patient and scrupulous hand.

Let us now consider the woman of the English novelist—because, alas, we are a nation of readers so insular that only a few thousands of us have heard of Madame Bovary and a very few hundreds of Lisa. Consequently, these figures hardly bulk at all as colouring the figure of the Woman of the Novelist as she affects us English.

Let us consider the best known woman of action in English imaginative writing; let us consider Portia. Here we have a woman witty a little beyond woman's wit: graceful a little beyond woman's grace: gracious a little beyond the graciousness of women: with a knowledge of the male heart a little beyond the knowledge that woman ever had. She is, in fact, the super-woman.

If we love Liza, we adore Portia: but if we believe in Turgenev's heroine do we ever quite believe in Shakespeare's? Do we ever quite—to the very back of our minds—believe in Cordelia? Or in Beatrice? Or in Desdemona? Or in Juliet? Do we believe that we shall ever meet with a woman like these ? And—what is more important still—do we ever believe that these women will " wear," that their qualities will not pall, their brilliances create in us no impatience, or cause in them no reactions that in their effects would try us beyond bearing ? Portia might get us out of a scrape : Juliet might answer passion with passion : Desdemona might bear with our ill-humours : Beatrice would pique us delightfully whilst we were courting. We might, in fact—we *do* certainly—believe in these super-women during certain stages of our lives. But . . . what a very big " But " that is !

And yet, with the women of Shakespeare the tradition of the Woman of the Novelist is already in full swing. This particular good woman—the heroine of an episode—is a peculiarly English product—a product of what Schopenhauer called, as we have said, Christo Germanisch Dummheit (Christo Germanic stupidity.) It is hardly, in fact, stupidity : it is rather idealism. (But then in the practical affairs of the world idealism is very nearly the same thing as stupidity.) The man, in fact, who would marry Beatrice would be a stupid man, or one obsessed by erotic idealism. (For certainly—quite certainly—she would " entrer dans son cabinet.")

Do not please imagine that these are mere cheapnesses. Or, if they are, consider how life itself is a matter of infinite cheapnesses. And then consider again how this tradition of the super-woman heroine

the woman who is the central figure of an episode—
has come right down to our own time on the wings of
the English novel. She is always, this super-woman,
gliding along some few inches above the earth, as we
glide when we dream we are flying. She is a sort of
Diana with triumphant mien before whose touch all
knotted problems dissolve themselves. So she has
traversed, this woman of the novelist, down and
across the ages until we find her, triumphant
and buoyant still, in the novels of Mr Meredith.
Do not we all adore Rose and Diana and Letty—
and all these other wonderful creatures? And do
not we all, at the back of our minds, disbelieve in
them?

You will say that Mr Meredith is the great painter
of your sex. But you will not believe that : the
statement is a product of emotion. You mean that
he is the great pleader for your sex.

Ah! the Woman of the Novelist—the Woman of
the Novelist : what great harm she has done to
the cause of women in these days and for centuries
back!

For consider what she has done : when Elizabethan
England put Portia on the stage the Elizabethan
Englishman considered that he had in public treated
Woman so handsomely that she had got as much as
she could reasonably expect. He proceeded in
private, to cheat her out of nine-tenths of what she
deserved.

You have only to read any of the innumerable

THE WOMAN OF THE NOVELISTS

" Advices to a Son," written by various Tudor gentlemen to realise to what an extent this was really the
case. The son was advised to regard his wife as a
very possibly—a very probably—dangerous adjunct
to a house. She was esteemed likely to waste a man's
substance, to cheat his heirs in the interests of an
almost inevitable second marriage. She was not to be
chosen for her talkativeness as that would distract a
man : (elle pourrait, in fact, entrer dans son cabinet)
She was not to be of a silent disposition because
she could not entertain him when he needed
entertainment.

And so—hardly and coldly—with that peculiar
hardness and coldness that distinguished all the
real manifestations of Tudor prudence — were the
lines of women's life laid down in these Tudor
testaments. Woman was a necessary animal, a
breeder of children ; but she was a very dangerous
one, or at least a very uncertain beast — a chest-
nut horse exhibited most of her characteristics.
Desdemona and the patient Grisel were acknow-
ledged to be dreams : Beatrice of the ready
tongue was to be eschewed, and as for Portia
— the Elizabethan was pretty sure, even *his*
lawyers with their settlements could not bind
her !

So that, in Elizabethan days, as to-day, you had a
Woman of the Novelists, a Super-Woman—set on
high and worshipped. But you had a very different
woman whom you contemplated—if you were a

L   161

man — from behind the locked doors of your *cabinet*.

To-day we have still the Woman of the Novelists— the woman of Mr Meredith. Like Portia she is inimitable in episodes : she will get a man out of a scrape : she will be inimitable too during a season of courtship. We do not, being English, go in for the novel of life : we do not want to : we do not want to face life. When we marry, it is a woman something like Portia, or Di Vernon, or Sophia Western, or Rose Harrington that we marry. We have given up as impracticable the Elizabethan habit of attempting, by selection or settlements, to choose and to tie down a partner for life. We have given it up ; we say : " The Woman of the Novelists is one thing ; but as for the woman we shall marry, she is an incomprehensible creature, bewildering and unknowable. We must take our chance."

But we should like to point out to you that we might say almost the same thing if we were going to make an indissoluble life-partnership with any man. We have, as it were, a romantic—a novelist's—idea that men, as distinguished from women, are upright, logical, hardworking, courageous, businesslike. We do not really believe this. But, if we go into partnership with a man, we do it because we like him or believe in him ; because, in fact, he appeals to us. We cannot tell how he will wear, any more than we can tell how the woman we marry,

or want to marry, will wear. He may go off with
the till : it may prove intolerable to sit day after
day in the same office with such a bounder ; the
fact that he comes in at night full of energy and
loquacity may be intolerable, too, if he is sharing
our rooms.

This will not much surprise us in a man. It
is apt to disconcert us very much in our Portia—
and we say : " What a strange beast woman is !
She was so clever with Shylock. Has not she
got the tact to see that we need our studies to ourselves ? "

Of course, the woman that we know, the woman,
that is to say, that eventually each of us gets to
know, is fused at last into the Woman of the Novelists.
This invariably happens, for we woo a Portia who has
neither a past nor a future, and life welds for us this
Portia into an ordinary woman. This combination
of the Woman of the Novelists who is always in one
note with a creature of much the same patiences,
impatiences, buoyant moments, reactions, morning
headaches and amiabilities, as our own—this hybrid
of a conventional deity and a quite real human being
is a very queer beast indeed. We wonder if you ever
quite realise what you are to the man on your hearthstone ? We do not know if any woman ever really
thinks—really—truly—and to the depths of her
whole being — thinks that she has a bad husband.
We do not know about this, but we are perfectly
certain that no husband ever thinks that he has a

bad wife. You see—poor, honest, muddled man
with the glamour of the novelist's woman on him—
he is always looking about somewhere in the odd and
bewildering fragments of this woman who has the
power to bedevil, to irritate, to plague and to madden
him. He looks about in this mist of personal contacts for the Cordelia that he still believes must be
there. He believes that his Sophia Western is still
the wise, tolerant, unjealous Sophia, who once made
him with the blessing of some Parson Adams, the
happiest of men. God forbid that we should say she
is not there. We are certain that the man believes she
is, only he cannot find her. He is so close to her, and
you know that if you hold your nose very close to a
carpet, it is useless to hope to see its pattern. But
no—believe us when we say that no man in the
silence of his study believes that he has a bad
wife. She may drink, but he will think that some
action, some attribute, or the circumstances of the
life that she has led with him, gives excuse.
She may nag, but he will believe that it is because
he has never really taken the trouble to explain
the excellencies of his motives and his actions.
She may be unfaithful, but in his heart he will
believe that it is because he has been unable to
maintain the strain of playing Benedick to her
Beatrice. And this poor, honest, simple man may
declaim against his wife to his friends, may seek
in new Amelias new disillusionments, may seek amid
the glamour of *causes celèbres* his liberty—but he will

listen to the words of his K.C.—of his special pleading conscience—with a certain contrition, for before his eyes, dimly radiant, there will stand the figure of the Woman of the Novelists.

Now, if this man never believes that his wife is a bad wife he will yet pick up certain little salient peculiarities. He will not believe that any given manifestation of unreasonableness is a part of the real character of his Di Vernon ; he will regard it as an accidental, as what Myers called a supra-liminal, exhibition, just as when he himself, having travelled first class with a third-class ticket, neglects to pay the excess fare. It is not the sort of thing he would do, it is only what by accident he has done. He remains honest and upright in spite of it. So when his wife calls him a beast he does not believe that the word " beast " is really a part of the vocabulary of, let us say, Dolly of the " Dolly Dialogues." It is all one with his excess fare that he carelessly—and it was so unlike him !—neglected to pay.

At the same time a constant aggregation of these little nothings becomes impressed upon his mind. They are the reaction from the Woman of the Novelists. He does not believe that they are part of his individual woman's nature, he cannot quite make them out—so he attributes them to her sex. (If he lived with a man he would not attribute them to this man's sex but he would say it was because poor so-and-so went to Eton instead of Winchester, or because he smokes too much, or because he takes after his parents.)

The woman of the music-hall, in fact—" My wife who won't let me " and " My wife's mother who has come to stay "—this creature is the direct product of *à rebours* of the Woman of the Novelists. For, if no man really believes that his wife is a woman of the music-hall, he is not so loyal to the wife of his friend Hunter. His own wife was *Diana of the Crossways*. She still, if she would only be serious for a minute—is Diana of the Crossways. Mrs Hunter, however, is only Mrs Hunter. To Hunter she was once St Catherine of Siena and still is saintly. But our friend catches certain phases of the intercourse of the Hunters; he hears an eloquent discourse of Hunter about the action of the tariff on the iron industry in Canada, he hears this eloquent and learned discourse interrupted by Mrs Hunter's description, let us say of the baby linen of the Prince of the Asturias. He does not know that Mrs Hunter was once St Catherine—is still St Catherine—and, as such, has a right to be more interested in infants than in iron trades. And, just as in the newspapers, crimes are recorded and the normal happenings of life let alone, so a number of irrational, unreasonable, illogical actions of real women become stored in our poor friend's mind. Thus he arrives at his grand question with which he will attempt to stump you, when you ask for a certain little something :

THE WOMAN OF THE NOVELISTS

" Why can't you," he asks, " learn to be logical, patient, businesslike, self-restrained ? "

" You cannot because of your sex ? Then give up talking and try to be the womanly woman."

And by the womanly woman he means the Woman of the Novelists. And if you achieved this impossibility, if you became this quite impossible she, he would still squash you with the unanswerable question :

" What does St Catherine, what on earth does St Catherine of Siena, want with a vote ? "

You see this terrible creation, this Woman of the Novelists has you both ways. Man has set her up to do her honour, and you, how foolishly and how easily you have fallen in the trap !—you, women, too, have aided and applauded this setting up of an empty convention. Women are not more illogical than men, but you are quite content as a rule to allow yourselves to be called illogical if only you may be called more subtle. Women are not less honourable cnan men, but you are quite content to be called less honourable than men if only you may be called long-suffering. In the interests of inflated virtues you have sacrificed the practical efficiencies of life, you are content to be called hysterical, emotional and utterly unworthy of a place in any decently ordered society, in order that you may let men bamboozle themselves into thinking that in other ways you are semi-divine. Well, this has recoiled upon your

own heads and now the average man, whilst believing
that in certain attributes you are semi-divine, believes
that in the practical things of this life you are more
incapable—the highest and most nearly divine of
you is more incapable of exercising the simplest
functions of citizenship than the lazy and incompetent brute who carries home your laundryman's
washing. I do not know which of you, woman or
novelist, is the more culpable. The novelist, being a
lazy brute, has evolved this convenient labour-saving
contrivance. You, thinking it would aid you in
maintaining an ascendancy over a gross and stupid
creature called man, have aided and abetted this
crime against the Arts, and the Arts have avenged
themselves, the gross and stupid creature has found
his account and you are left as the Americans say
" in the cart."

Whether there will ever come a reaction, the God
Who watches over all to-morrows alone can tell.
But you have the matter a great deal in your own
hands, for to such an extent is the writer of imaginative literature dependent on your suffrages, that if
women only refused to read the works of any writer
who unreasonably idealises their sex, such writers
must starve to death. For it should be a self-evident
proposition that it would be much better for you to
be, as a sex, reviled in books. Then men coming to
you in real life would find how delightful you actually
are, how logical, how sensible, how unemotional, how
capable of conducting the affairs of the world. For

we are quite sure that you are, at least we are quite sure that you are as capable of conducting them as are men in the bulk. That is all we can conscientiously say and all, we feel confident, that you will demand of us.

MODERN POETRY

CHAPTER VIII

MODERN POETRY

WE make a mistake in looking too eagerly for the figure of the great poet as the one necessity of a poetical school. And when we lament to-day that we have neither a Tennyson nor a Browning, we lament too early and too casually. Let us consider for a moment the case of poetry rather than the case of the poet. It is possibly true that, at the present time, we have among us no figure that is very monumental. We write this with some diffidence, for at any moment a giant may loom upon the horizon. But if, at the present moment, we have no very great figure, this would only go to show that now—as should be the case—the art of poetry is in sympathy with the spirit of the age. If we have no great figure in poetry we have no great figure any_where. And, with the exception of one or two very old men, the survivors of a time when the great figure flourished as never before, there are few to be found in the whole world. This may be because we have lost the sense of reverence. There may, that is to say, be amongst us half a dozen poets as great as Tennyson. There may be half a dozen, and we may simply have lost the power to appreciate them. And it must be remembered that the great figure flourished and expanded not so much on account of his technical qualities as on account of his moral worth. The great figure was, as a rule, a long-bearded person of a wind-blown aspect. He commanded respect—he insisted upon it—not because he was going to give pleasure by the beauty of his words or the music of his periods, but because he was a sort of moral alchemist. He cared comparatively little whether or not he gave our fathers pleasure : he was going to solve the riddle of the universe. Upon the whole he was a rather disagreeable man, and, if we are glad that we came into contact with such in some numbers during our early years, we are quite certain that we are very much more glad that they no longer exist. There is, that is to say, no longer any necessity for us (or for any one else) to stand nervous and trembling, like a schoolboy in the presence of his headmaster, before some enormous creature with an outline resembling that of a snow-mountain, and in our heart a terrible fear of precipitating a torrent of moral indignation upon our head by praising some rival. For in the days of our fathers the moral note was always to the fore. If one great figure fulminated against another, it was not because his work was bad, but because it showed vicious tendencies. Thus Mr Ruskin would abuse a painter who had injured him, not because his drawing was faulty, but because his line showed evidence of a corrupt mind. In an almost similar vein Count

MODERN POETRY

Tolstoi declared that the music of Wagner was unclean and that Maupassant's prose defiled the ear. We have got beyond that stage, at any rate as far as poetry in England is concerned. On the other hand, there is no doubt that the poet has altogether lost the ear of the public. This is inevitable, because the public in England, being exclusively utilitarian, demands of all the Arts that they shall either render the individual a better shopkeeper by adding to his knowledge, or that they shall improve his chances of getting to heaven and his feeling of self-righteousness.

A great many things have gone to the abolition of the moral standpoint as a factor in modern verse. For one thing, the poet having developed a sense of humour, no longer takes himself with a seriousness altogether preposterous. For another, the poet has become more sincere : he writes, that is to say, along the lines of his own personality and of his own personal experience. He does very much less generalising from the works of contemporary Scientists, Divines, and Social Reformers. Great poetry—poetry with the note of greatness—would seem to demand a simplicity of outlook upon a life not very complex. The poet is a creature of his emotions, and seldom or never is his intellect very powerful or very steady. For there can be no doubt that the more emotional play there is demanded of a man's brain the less rigidity will it have for the following of logical thought-trains. Thus, the last really great poet working in a really complex age may be said to have been

THE CRITICAL ATTITUDE

Lucretius. To Dante the digesting of all the knowledge in the world was a comparatively simple matter. And having assimilated it he could write fearlessly, with assurance, and with composure. With the flood of new knowledges let loose upon the world by the Renaissance, and with the rendering of these knowledges accessible by means of the printing press, the task of mastering all that could be known grew appreciably more difficult, and Shakespeare was probably the last of the great poets to work in a day when wisdom was a really practicable matter. For to be wise—or rather, to write with the assurance that he is so, and with the determination and the skill to convince the reader of his wisdom—a poet must have the comfortable belief either that he knows everything, or that he knows where to go easily to gain his information. And gallant or obtuse souls who imagined that at least they were potentially all-wise have remained with us through the ages until the passing away of the last Victorian great figure, until nearly the end of the first decade of the present century. Until then the poet regarded himself as the philosopher, as the theologian, as the counsellor of humanity. Shelley was the poet of atheism. Montgomery Smith chanted the Christian virtues, Longfellow was the bard of Puritan perfections, Tennyson in his poems sought to give us a theory of constructive Pantheism, Sir Lewis Morris sang of Hell, Sir Edwin Arnold was a Buddhist. These, of course, are ill-assorted names, but they go to show how from the day when Milton wrote " Paradise Lost " until just yesterday, in all strata and in all its varieties, poetry and prophecy went hand in hand. And, as we have said, the public looks to its poets to be also its prophets. There is only one poet living who has ever appealed to the British public with a sort of clarion note such as was the Tennyson's of " Riflemen Form." And it is characteristic that this poet, Mr Kipling, appealed to the same set of emotions. This set of emotions— those of patriotism, of voluntary service, and of simple physical aggression—probably remain dormant and ready to the hand of any writer with sufficient technical skill to awaken them. Mr Kipling came exceedingly near being a great poet. Moreover, he is so exceedingly near to a supreme verbal skill, and so exceedingly near to the power of using the rhythm of music as only a genius can, that Mr Kipling may yet—for all I should care to dogmatise—stand out as the representatively national figure amongst a band of singers as numerous, and as intimately satisfactory, as were ever the minor Elizabethans and the early Jacobeans. Mr Kipling as a poet has never been regarded with very much critical attention, though his popularity was at one time as unboundedly swelling as it now is, rather unreasonably, on the wane. He is to be commended as much for his boldness in the use of the vernacular, as for his skill and his boldness, too, in catching the rhythm of popular music, with its quaint and fascinating irregularities.

But, with the exception of Mr Kipling, there is no

poet to-day who attempts successfully to sing of patriotism or any of the other eternal verities. And it is characteristic of the age that the poetry upon which Mr Kipling built the platform for verse of such bland popularity as " The Absent-minded Beggar "— the poetry which put him in a position to become a prophet, was poetry not of a patriotic or of a national character—was poetry not even of a military type, but was the poetry of intimacy. Thus " On the Road to Mandalay " expressed not heroic resolve, not the determination to die for England, but the nostalgia of an individual.

And so it is with all the poetry of to-day. We are producing, not generalisations from facts more or less sparse, but the renderings of the moods of many individuals. For the trouble to-day with the poet, as with all the rest of the world, is that we know too much. We know so much, we know so many little things that we are beginning to realise how much there is in the world to know, and how little of all that there is, is the much that we know. Thus there is an end of generalisations.

And we must confess that for us this is a matter of the profoundest satisfaction. This may be a sympton of degeneracy, but we prefer to regard it as a portent of a new birth. For us—and we presume for a great many other people—literature is hardly so much a matter of books as of the personalities that the books reveal to us. And, in the enormous quantity of modern verse that has passed through our hands in the last few years, we have become acquainted with a number nearly as vast of small intimate shades of personalities. This has been to us a matter of very great satisfaction. Instead, that is to say, of making the acquaintance of two or three enormous poets like Tennyson or Rossetti, whom one suspected always of posing, of forcing the poetic note, of giving not so much what they intimately liked as what they regarded as appropriate for a poet to like—instead of these few great figures we have made the acquaintance of a number—of a whole circle—of smaller, more delicate, and more exquisite beings.

Of Victorian poetry we must confess to liking really only a few poems of Browning's and a very considerable number of Christina Rossetti's. Indeed, with her intimate and searching self-revelations, with her exquisite and precise language, Christina Rossetti seems to us to be the most valuable poet that the Victorian age produced. She dealt hardly at all in ideas : nearly every one of her poems was an instance, was an illustration of an emotion. And this, it seems to us, is the mood in which, if we are to get anything out of Modern Poetry, we must approach it. Until modern knowledge has been reduced to knowledge-ability—until, that is to say, biology, astronomy, ethics, social and political economics, the history of England, and the Poor Law system—until all the sciences have been so crystallised by specialists that one poet may be able to take them all in, and until we have that one poet, we cannot have any more poetry of the great manner. For the great manner demands a certain conceit on the part of its practitioner; the little patches, which are all that to-day we can grasp, are sufficient only to make any reasonable man more humble. And the poet must be a man instinct with a certain sweet reasonableness that permits him to grasp at truth to the measure of the light vouchsafed him. It is thus possible that the Muse in the effort to produce the next great poet is only taking breath for an effort almost supreme. She may very well—in the course of who knows what time ?—produce another author of another " De Natura Rerum," dealing, however, with things upon a scale infinitely more vast than was ever to be approached even by Lucretius. But that will scarcely be in our day, and for us the image of the poetic art is like that of the shrine in Cologne Cathedral. For we seem to see as many as would be non-miraculously visible of eleven thousand virgin poets sheltering under the cloak of a St Ursula. And the St Ursula has the features of the authoress of " Goblin Market."

It would, of course, be superfluous to say that this is no more than an image, or to explain that we are not trying to say that Mr Newbolt, let us say, is a son spiritually or technically of Christina Rossetti. But Christina Rossetti was a symptom of what would happen in the age that has succeeded that of the Victorian giants. She suffered, as it were, a similar martyrdom—she lived amongst giants with extraordinarily loud voices. Mr Ruskin shouted at her that her poems were a young lady's work and had much better not be published. D. G. Rossetti, the Pre-Raphaelites, and other great figures filled all the reception-rooms of her house, used up all the clean paper, and chanted very loudly, whilst, using the backs of envelopes upon the corner of her bedroom wash-handstand, Christina Rossetti wrote her poems.

> ". . . Like poor Dan Robin thankful for your crumb,
> Whilst other birds sang mortal loud like swearing,
> When the wind lulled she tried to get a hearing."

And this is very much the position of Modern Poetry now. It is true that we have to-day no Ruskins, but we have—this is a democratic age !—a body of reviewers who with one voice chant always the truism : " There is no great figure." Patriotism is taken in hand by the music-halls : Love has been extinguished by Mr Bernard Shaw and his disciples ; Christianity, Pity, and the older virtues are in the hands of Dr Clifford, Mr Galsworthy, the Editor of the *British Weekly*, and a similarly composed group of earnest persons. Thus the great figure has been replaced by groups. And although groups cannot, with all their multiplicity of hands, write " A Red Cotton Night-cap Country," although no twelve earnest men together can provide us with a great poem, they can very well, each group apart representing Patriotism, Love, Pity, and the Christian Virtues—speaking as it were not like Pontiffs, but like Œcumenical Councils vested with authority, gravely let the public know that Modern

THE CRITICAL ATTITUDE

Poetry in their eyes (as was Christina Rossetti's in the eyes of Mr Ruskin) is a negligible, young-ladyish thing that will do no harm, but that had better not be published.

But, as a matter of fact, Modern Poetry is a thing not very sturdy, but extraordinarily tenacious of life. We have not got any great poet, but we have an extraordinary amount of lyrical ability. And this is a very healthy sign. Music in England fell upon evil days as soon as it dropped into the hands of the professional musician. Before the days of Handel and Buononcini as we have pointed out, every gentleman could handle a lute and take part in a four-voiced concert, composing his notes for himself as he went along. This was then as much a part of a liberal education as to-day is a careful attention to the halfpenny press. And this was a more healthy state for the Art of Music than is the listening to a gentleman with sinews of iron, a remarkable wind, and an extraordinary memory for musical phrases. In just the same way, cricket and football were more beneficial to the nation and flourished better themselves before what is called the era of professionalism. And upon the whole there is, nowadays, more good poetry written in the course of a year than there was when the great figure flourished in Victorian days. It is only a very small proportion of the work of Lord Tennyson, of Browning, of Swinburne, of Rossetti, or of the late Mr Meredith that will really stand the test of time, since it is only very seldom that these

MODERN POETRY

writers are—or that any writer is—at the very best.
Now almost every man has in him the writing of one
good poem. Just for once emotion will produce in
him sincerity and a gift of expression lasting for a few
minutes. Thus with the extension of technical
ability, and above all with the extension of desire for
expression, we are enormously widening the net. We
are approaching, in fact, once more to a state such as
that which produced ballads and folk-songs, those productions of the utterly obscure and of the utterly
forgotten. Ballads and folk-songs are never Great
Poetry, but what exquisite pleasure they can give us,
and what a light they can throw upon the human heart!
And that, in essence, must be the province of Modern
Poetry for some time to come—to give pleasure and
to throw light upon the human heart. The verse
which of late years has caused us the most exquisite
of pleasures —we are not holding it up critically,
ex cathedra, as the finest poem that has ever been
written—is the following :—

AN EPITAPH

" Here lies a most beautiful lady,
　　Light of heart and step was she ;
　　I think she was the most beautiful lady
　　That ever was in the West Country.
　　But beauty vanishes, beauty passes,
　　However rare, rare it be,
　　And when I crumble who shall remember
　　That lady of the West Country ? "

For the purposes of our argument we will refrain from
giving the name of the writer, who, at the time we

read the poem in manuscript, was quite unknown to us, and who is now no more than a mere nodding acquaintance. We read this poem once in manuscript and once in proof for sub-editorial purposes, and having thus read it twice, after more than two years we remember it so exactly as to be able to write it down letter-perfect except for the fact that the author has preferred to spell " Country," " Countrie." Thus we seem to have all ready for the Bishop Percy of the future an excellent folk-ballad. As to its intrinsic value we cannot dogmatise. It has afforded us, in its kind, the highest pleasure of which we are capable. We do not know why this is, but we are absolutely convinced of the fact. It touches us as much as the words :—

> " O waly, waly, gin luve be bonnie
> A little while when it is new :
> When it grows old it waxes cold
> And fades away like morning dew.
>
> And had I wist before I kissed
> That luve had been sae ill to win,
> I had locked my heart in a kist of gold
> And pinned it wi' a siller pin."

These verses also we have only read once—we do not very well remember where. We strongly suspect them of being part of what is called a " fake-ballad." But in any case they have given us more pleasure than any other ballad in the Percy " Reliques." They represent the most intimate personal feelings of a passionate nature, just as Mr Walter de la Mare's— the name has slipt out, and there let it remain—just as Mr Walter de la Mare's poem expresses, with an exquisite intimacy, an emotion of a nature contemplative and attractive.

We do not mean to say that if we search through the many small volumes of poems that are being published during these present years we should find any very huge portion of entirely exquisite poetry : but we are convinced that we should dredge up a sufficiency in the course of a century or so, to make several very creditable volumes of " Reliques." And this alone is a sufficient justification for the Muse whose business it is to provide for the delectation of men of goodwill, not figures, but poetry.

And this is a very profound truth, not a mere paradox. For to-day we produce not so many great lives as an infinite flicker of small vitalities. If we had looked from our window a hundred years ago at the night upon the great western-going highway that is now, and was then, beneath them, we should have seen eight times every hour, galloping hard down the hill from the turnpike at the top, through the darkness against the black timber of the park opposite, four horses with lamplight on their shining limbs, their harness and their traces. There would have been the loom of the figures of the coachman and the outside passengers. Very dimly to be made out there would be the shapeless forms of the luggage beneath the tarpaulin, and there would have risen up thin and fine amidst the rattle of hoofs the sound of the guard's horn. This might have been seen eight times an hour during the day and the night, and there would have been those definite things to catch hold of or to make a song about.   But looking out upon the same highway during the twilight of to-day, one sees, as it were, innumerable motes of life in a settled stream, in a never-ceasing stream, in a stream that seems as if it must last for ever.   And for us we are glad that we live to-day, that we did not die when the coaches went by and the horns blew.   It is perfectly true that the coach would have seemed to bulk larger upon the road, to be an individuality more important, to be, as it were, a great figure.   It had more personality, but infinitely less of delicacy, and there seems to us to be so much more of poetry in all the little lights that whirl past, in the shadows that flicker, in the tenuous and momentary reflections seen in the polish of carriage panels—in the impersonality of it all.   And all these impressions are so fragile, so temporary, so evanescent, that the whole stream of life appears to be a procession of very little things, as if, indeed, all our modern life were a dance of midges.

And indeed all our modern life is a dance of midges. We know no one very well, but we come into contact with an infinite number of people ; we stay nowhere very long, but we see many, many places.   We have hardly ever time to think long thoughts, but an infinite number of small things are presented for our cursory reflections.   And in all of it—in all of this gnats' dance of ours—there is a note of mournfulness, of resignation, of poetry.

MODERN POETRY

And if we have a quarrel with modern verse, it is that it too little reflects this tenuous poetry of our own day. Most of the verse that is written to-day deals in a derivative manner with mediæval emotions. This means that the poets have not the courage to lead their own lives. They seem to shut themselves up in quiet book-cabinets, to read for ever, and to gain their ideas of life for ever from some very small, very specialised group of books, or to dream for ever of islands off the west coast of Ireland.

It is a charming thing, it is a very lovely thing, it is a restful thing, to lose ourselves in meditations upon the Isles of the Blessed, and very sweet songs may be sung about them. But to do nothing else implies a want of courage. We live in our day, we live in our time, and he is not a proper man who will not look in the face his day and his time. It is to cast down our little shield and short sword, to run from the battle, and to hide for ever at Tusculum. And this frame of mind is a bad one, not because it matters very much what class of subjects a poet deals in. There is no particular reason why a gentleman living upon Chelsea Embankment should not write about Paolo and Francesca ; but if he have never lived and never loved, himself, if he have never known passion or danger, he will never realise that Paolo and Francesca loved and suffered precisely as love and suffer the inhabitants of the flat above him. He must feel that when Richard I. was king, the leaves blew from off the trees along the drifting smoke of autumn fires, just as to-day, reluctantly, at the back of the house, the foliage loosens its grasp upon the tall poplars to fall in showers, in blown bee-swarms, into the gutters of the opposite houses, and into the mud of the mews. For, if the poet is timid in his life, he will be shrinking in his thoughts and over-delicate in his words. He will express, not himself, but himself as he would like to appear to other gentlemen who have read the " Divina Comedia " and the works of the minor pre-Raphaelite poets. There is, of course, no reason why a gentleman should not indulge in these elegant pastimes ; on the contrary, they may do some good by remembering, and so assuaging, the sufferings of many poor souls in purgatory. For, no doubt, one of the chiefest sufferings of the dead is oblivion. And the cultivated gentleman who discovers in some record that Cina da Pistoia had an uncle, and who thereupon indites a sestina to the memory of Cina da Pistoia's relative, may afford that poor ghost some moments of comfort. But of these acts of piety, of these disinterrings of the forgotten, and these idealisings of a past which in its day was no more romantic than is our own time, of these settings wrong of perspective we have enough always with us. And these times and climes have been so well sung by their own contemporaries and inhabitants. Horace wrote of the vulgarities of the Via Flaminia very much as Mr W. B. Yeats might write of Hampstead Heath. His soul shuddered at it. Nevertheless, even Horace was a Roman of his day and time,

MODERN POETRY

and found material in his own vulgar epoch for verse
which is charming enough. We go, in the end, to
our poets to be told something—either of how the
poet's friends and enemies lived, or of how he was
affected by his contact with them, by his views of cities
and plains, or by his twenty-five-year wooing of a
married lady unfortunately indifferent to him. But
we go to him in any case for his real self. And unless
he speaks to us sincerely, without affectation, and in
such language as he ordinarily uses, his poems will ring
false, and we shall find little pleasure in him. A
further attribute poets must have if their work is to
have any real appeal to their age : they must be in
some sympathy with their fellow men. Personally
I should care very little for the fact that poetry in
particular, and literature in general, have lost all
appeal to the public ear—I should care very little if
this were not a symptom that the disease of Dilettan-
tism has crept into, has almost overwhelmed, the brains
of the great body of modern poets. That the public
should " guy " good poetry is a healthy sign ; that
it should call Shelley an atheist or Browning an im-
postor was natural and, in its way, excellent. But
the poets should have lost even the power to irritate
the lethargic beast—this is a symptom of a lamentable impotence on the part of the poets. The receding
influence of the great figure, of the moral purpose,
things of the past, is however still strong. It is waning,
but there are still too many small people in authority
who, standing in the folds of the mantle of the de-

parted Great, are ready to cry at the slightest poetic stir : " There is no great figure."

So that originality of handling or courage of conviction have hardly as yet had time to gather themselves together. But that one day a stirring of the pool will come we need have no doubt. And it will come when some young poets get it into their heads to come out of their book-closets and take, as it were, a walk down Fleet Street, or a ride on the top of a 'bus from Shepherd's Bush to Poplar. We are using, of course, these peregrinations metaphorically. It does not much matter where the poet goes or what he does, so long as he turns inquiring, sincere, and properly humble eyes upon the life that is around him. In that case poetry would come entirely into its own again. It will become once more human nature's daily food, instead of being, as it is now, the sweet liqueur at the end of a banquet, or chocolates in the little crystal bowls that nestle neglected amongst green smilax upon the tablecloth. For it is a mistake to say that the Englishman does not read poetry. He reads it, he craves for it, he cannot get on without it ; it saves him the trouble of thinking, and that is why his conversation is usually rounded off with a catchword from the Holy Scriptures or a misquotation from Shakespeare. Only the poet, to secure this misquotation, must be sincere—whether in wisdom or in folly matters little.